# BUY HIGH, SELL HIGHER

# BUY HIGH, SELL HIGHER

## WHY BUY-AND-HOLD IS DEAD AND OTHER INVESTING LESSONS FROM CNBC'S "THE LIQUIDATOR"

### JOE TERRANOVA

BUSINESS
PLUS

NEW YORK   BOSTON

The information in this book is as up to date and as accurate as possible. However, it is sold with the understanding that markets are unpredictable, and risk is an inherent part of investing. The author and publisher specifically disclaim any liability which is incurred from the use or application of the contents of this book.

All stock charts courtesy of CNBC Pro.

Business Plus
Hachette Book Group
237 Park Avenue
New York, NY 10017
www.HachetteBookGroup.com

Printed in the United States of America

RRD-C

First Edition: January 2012

Business Plus is an imprint of Grand Central Publishing.

The Business Plus name and logo are trademarks of Hachette Book Group, Inc.

The Hachette Speakers Bureau provides a wide range of authors for speaking events. To find out more, go to www.hachettespeakersbureau.com or call (866) 376-6591.

The publisher is not responsible for websites (or their content) that are not owned by the publisher.

10   9   8   7   6   5   4   3   2   1

Library of Congress Cataloging-in-Publication Data

Terranova, Joe.
   Buy high, sell higher : why buy-and-hold is dead and other investing lessons from CNBC's "The Liquidator" / Joe Terranova.—1st ed.
      p. cm.
   ISBN 978-1-4555-0066-6
   1. Investments.   2. Speculation.   3. Investment analysis.   I. Title.
   HG4521.T43 2012
   332.6—dc23
                                  2011041600

*In the chest pocket of my trading floor jacket,
written on a small pit trading card I kept and
shared with my traders, was the following mantra:*

*"For 365 days a year, it's game 7."*

*This book is dedicated to all those people who
incorporate that mantra into their lives.*

*Tucker, Tanner, and Remy: Mommy and
I hope that is how you will live your lives.*

# Contents

Don't try to Buy & Sell
according to what you think
Katrina will do — That is
gambling — wait until it
happens — then buy &
sell accordingly — plant &
this

eg. B C E    short
— privileges either & go short
big day — then buy

# Prologue

## Investing Lessons from Hurricane Katrina

M*illions of dollars were on the line.*

It was Monday, August 22, 2005, and it seemed as if only one news story mattered that week: a hurricane named Katrina was barreling toward the Gulf Coast. Of course, a week before the storm made landfall at New Orleans, no one knew that it would become the costliest natural disaster in American history. On the twenty-second, Katrina was just another storm.

MBF, my employer at the time, was and still is one of the biggest natural gas and oil trading firms in the world. For professional investors, disasters and other major global events provide opportunities in which fortunes can be won or lost. For example, in 1992, George Soros famously risked $10 billion when he shorted the British pound. The British government had insisted that it would not devalue the British sterling, but Soros was skeptical. On September 16, 1992, a day that would become known as Black Wednesday, he bet $10 billion against the pound. Soros was right, and he made a profit of $958 million in a single day (and a total of $2 billion from all of his investments against the pound at that time).

Of course, Soros hasn't been the only one to capitalize on others' misfortunes. As early as 2005, hedge fund manager John

Paulson spotted an impending disaster and a great opportunity developing in the U.S. housing market. Paulson and his team's foresight led them to make the greatest trade in financial history, and in 2007 Paulson made a staggering $15 billion by shorting the housing market. However, for every career-making success, there are those investing ideas that destroy fortunes and break firms.

As Katrina approached the United States, my colleagues at MBF and I were not willing to take a Soros- or Paulson-sized position on whether the storm would hit or miss New Orleans. Instead, our plan was to stay on the sidelines. What we did at MBF in August 2005 holds a less dramatic but far more useful lesson for the average investor than Soros's and Paulson's profitable plays.

In August 2005, neither my boss, MBF's owner, Mark Fisher, nor I was trying to figure out some intricate plan to profit from the hurricane. We were not going to play the hurricane, but we needed to make sure that the storm didn't play us. It's important to understand that when a large market event hits, volatility spikes. In most instances, the retail investor doesn't have the ability to navigate through that volatility. A professional trader does, but most retail investors simply do not know what to do in a situation like that. That's why individual investors often lose money in an event like Katrina. The professionals understand that at times like Katrina, it's not about making money; it's about preserving capital.

In the days leading up to the storm, Mark was looking at the big picture, attempting to calculate the impact of the hurricane on the structure of the energy market. The goal was to reduce our risk—to manage our risk first—which is what the vast majority of investors don't understand. Manage your risk first, and you are sure to come back to fight another day. That's the number one priority with something as big as Katrina—or even with something as small as a quarterly earnings report from a company in which you own stock.

In summer 2005, with Hurricane Katrina looming, if any trader had a large position in natural gas and the market went against him, he would have been forced to liquidate his position and take a substantial loss. Being forced into a decision is not a winning investment strategy. Nobody has a sustainable track record of profits when they're forced by the market to make a decision. The investors who are successful are those who avoid having their decisions dictated by the market. The best traders make their own decisions and do not allow outside events to force their hand.

Hurricane Katrina posed two potential outcomes that worried us. In a hurricane, most people incorrectly assume that the price of oil spikes because of the threat of an impending shortage. That's wrong, though, because the president simply could release oil from the strategic petroleum reserve to satisfy the need for oil. It's not oil that matters. It's gasoline, a by-product of oil which is produced in refineries. Refineries are littered throughout the Gulf Coast. And what do refineries need? They need electrical power to run them. They also need to remain dry. So the two worst things that could happen to refineries are that they lose power and they flood.

If the hurricane hit, the prices of gasoline, heating oil, and natural gas would skyrocket because the pipelines would have to be shut, creating a scarcity of those commodities. In that instance, had an investor been "long" oil (meaning that investors expected prices to rise), he would have made a great deal of money after the hurricane did its damage in the Gulf. Had the hurricane missed, then the prices of those same commodities would have fallen by a significant margin once that risk was taken out of the market.

My title at MBF was director of trading. One of my many responsibilities was to manage risk and to make sure that we never bet the firm on a single trade or event. I had seventy-five proprietary traders putting the firm's money to work plus junior traders and interns—about three hundred team members reported to me in all. I was dubbed the "Liquidator" because everyone knew that when I showed up on the trading floor, located at the World Financial Center right on the Hudson River, my job was to get a trader out of a particular position by selling large blocks of a particular asset. This happened frequently, almost always when one of our traders was down a lot of money and just could not pull the trigger to take his losses and preserve his capital. However, my job entailed more than simply selling commodities or securities. My job had a technical side, too. Mark entrusted me to see the big picture and to ensure that the firm's risk was properly allocated.

The toughest part of my job was taking a trader out of the game. Like a baseball team manager relieving a starting pitcher and taking him off the mound, my job was to take that trader out of the pit. It wasn't always easy, and taking a trader out of the pit often meant tense moments for both of us. Still, I loved my job, and I never forgot how far I had come: I had grown up in Valley Stream, Long Island, a working-class town just a few miles outside of the superwealthy Five Towns community. As a kid, I needed to hold down three paper routes—for *Newsday*, the *Mail Leader* (a local paper), and the *Daily News*—in order to have some spending money. Now I held a leadership position in one of the great trading firms in the country—a firm that was headed for a potential crisis unless I was able to effectively protect its coffers from overeager traders trying to bet big on an uncertain event.

Aside from keeping an eye on what our traders were doing that morning, I needed to understand their mental state. And the mental state of most of my traders leading up to Katrina was lousy, to say the least.

Katrina was scheduled to make landfall on August 29, the Monday morning after what is known among my colleagues as "Guilt Week"—the week between the end of summer camp and the start of the school year (Guilt Week started on August 22 that year). This was the week when all of the dads and moms who hadn't spent much time with their children all summer took the week off to be with their families, flocking to beaches and other kid-friendly destinations.

However, Guilt Week was just a part of the story. Our traders also were away from the trading pits because they had grown increasingly frustrated with the price of natural gas and its inability to reach the milestone price of $10 per BTU (or British thermal unit, a measurement of heat created by burning a material). As it was, on one of the most potentially profitable trading days of the year, August 22, most of our traders had decided to take the week off.

So, when news of a potential hurricane hit the wires on that Monday, the twenty-second, the oil and natural gas trading pits were eerily quiet. For weeks, our traders expected the price of natural gas to top $10, but it never happened. It didn't really matter why gas wasn't topping $10—it could have been for any number of reasons, any of them right or wrong. The point was that it just could not get there. As a result, even though our traders knew that searching for a valid reason to explain the price of gas was a fool's errand, they were a frustrated group. I knew this firsthand because my eldest son was christened the week before at St. Joseph's Church in Hewlett, Long Island. All our traders attended the reception at Carltun on the Park but did little else there but complain about the price of natural gas. Most of them sold all their natural gas positions and decided to go on what felt to them like a forced vacation during Guilt Week.

With most of our A-team at the beach, news of a possible hurricane ignited a new bull market in natural gas that Monday. Natural gas closed that day at $9.564 after hitting a low of $9.032 and a high of $9.840. The price of natural gas fluctuated 80 cents (or 8½ percent) that day—a significant percentage for a commodity trading under $10. That only made things worse because my traders had been waiting for weeks for the price of natural gas to pop, and the first day they stepped away from the pits, the price surged. The traders already were discouraged, and then this once-in-a-decade event happened. Because most of the spouses of our traders knew almost nothing about trading, they couldn't have cared less whether natural gas was trading at $10. This forced our traders to internalize the pain, since there was no one at home they could talk to about what was happening back at work.

When word spread of the hurricane, our traders could not get back to the trading pits fast enough—Guilt Week or not. But it took most of our traders until Wednesday—two or three days since the price of natural gas spiked—to return from wherever they had taken their families. When they got back to the office, they were all in foul moods. They were an ornery group when they left and even more ornery when they returned. The fragile state of our traders' egos required a particular kind of leadership. I had to be their priest, rabbi, and psychologist all at the same time. This meant dozens of one-on-one sessions during which I could talk these traders off the cliff edge and assure them that all would work out well in the end. I always did this in their favorite places, their home turfs, whether it was their favorite bagel shop or sushi restaurant, or wherever they felt most comfortable. I explained to them that I understood their pain while simultaneously helping them to look past the present to a more favorable future that I knew would be there as long as they were able to improve their attitudes and change their mind-sets.

These counseling sessions served as yet another reminder about the connection between emotions and trading. When a trader gets out of rhythm mentally, he loses his balance. He often becomes focused on the upside, not on what he could lose. It's easy for him to forget that he needs to protect his downside first. Our conversations were not so much about what could be made during Katrina, but on what could be lost. I encouraged my traders to consider the worst-case scenario of every potential trade.

The price of natural gas hadn't hit $10 in about two years, so those traders who were most bullish on natural gas took this as an omen that a huge breakout was in the offing. Since many of our traders had been bullish on natural gas, they would have made a great deal of money that Monday, just trading for the day. That was one of the contributing factors that caused them the most pain. They all knew they could have bought in at just over $9 and had many opportunities to sell up to $9.80. By Tuesday, August 23, it was clear that the hurricane had the potential to destroy vital oil assets in the Gulf. If that happened—if there were a direct hit on the oil platforms and refineries—the price of oil and natural gas would skyrocket. However, we knew that approximately two out of every three hurricanes usually fizzled out; they usually missed the most vital targets. That was the main reason many of our traders—even some who had been bullish on natural gas—wanted to short natural gas before the hurricane swept through the Gulf (once the hurricane missed, the price of oil and natural gas would drop immediately and by a large percentage). Managing traders during times like these can be a challenge, and Katrina was no exception.

On that Wednesday, August 24, the price of natural gas finally traded above $10 during the day, but it closed at $9.98. That Friday, seventy-two hours before the storm hit, natural gas once again rose to $10, trading at an intraday high of $10.07. However, natural gas could not sustain that price, and it closed at $9.79 that day. That price told me that most traders did not expect the storm to hit and damage key infrastructure in the Gulf. Had more traders expected a direct hit of the storm, the price would have closed significantly higher than $10.

One of the things that I was so focused on that week, and what I wanted my traders to understand, was that it did not matter to me what their profit-and-loss statements looked like on Monday morning (August 29). Trading or investing should not be reduced to guesswork, which is exactly what would have happened had I allowed traders to bet their hunches on this potential hurricane. I had a lot of guys say to me on that Friday, "If this is a dud, let's short the market, because we're going to make a lot of money." I knew intuitively that this was precisely the worst way to view this event.

Instead, my job was to get my traders to look past the moment and understand the big picture. Instead of allowing them to play their hunches, I made them liquidate their positions before the storm hit, because we just didn't know what was going to happen. The only thing we could be sure of was that when the storm rendered its verdict on Monday morning, there would be an imbalance in the energy market one way or the other. I wanted my traders to have plenty of ammunition in order to take advantage of the opportunities that surely would be created. If the hurricane made landfall in Louisiana and Texas, it would take out refineries along the way and cause a huge shift upward in the price of natural gas that could go on for months, creating great weeks of opportunities for our traders. If it missed, the price would take a nosedive and likely return to its pre-Katrina equilibrium. However, taking any significant position before Katrina made landfall would constitute gambling, and gambling and trading are never the same thing.

Many people erroneously equate gambling with trading, but successful traders never gamble on their investments. Traders can calculate risk based on a potential outcome or, in this case, a price direction based on historical data. In addition, professional traders are astute at price pattern recognition (the movement of assets based on similar events from the past). Many good traders have photographic memories. They can remember seeing similar price movements in the market and correlating it back so they'll know how to trade if history does repeat itself. That is what separates traders from gamblers. Good traders wait for opportunities that they can identify as a result of their experience and knowledge honed by years of observing the capital markets. In contrast, most gamblers throw caution to the wind and usually just guess on how something will come out.

On the Friday before the storm hit land, my job was to make absolutely sure that my traders had position flexibility the following week. I knew come Monday there would be thousands of traders, less disciplined than the MBF team, who had guessed wrong and would be forced to liquidate. I wanted my guys to be in a position to take advantage of the opportunity that was going to exist when others were being forced to liquidate their losing positions.

I knew that if the hurricane hit vital assets in the Gulf, then the $10 natural gas target would be blown away. Fortunately, we were able successfully to liquidate hundreds of contracts before the storm hit.

Today we know that the storm was the most violent in history and wreaked a huge amount of damage on the oil platforms and other key infrastructure. That caused the price of natural gas (and other oil products) to surge by more than 20 percent to $12 the first trading day after Katrina hit. Had I allowed our traders to keep their short positions, it would have wiped out much of the traders' year-to-date profits. (One hedge fund, the now-defunct Amaranth, originally played Katrina correctly, but then tried to repeat that success during the 2006 hurricane season by wagering the entire firm on energy contracts, leading to losses of more than $6 billion when that storm failed to strike the Gulf Coast and the price of natural gas fell more than 20 percent. Amaranth was wiped out by that play.)

Because MBF was liquid going into the event, Hurricane Katrina created a great trading environment for the rest of the year

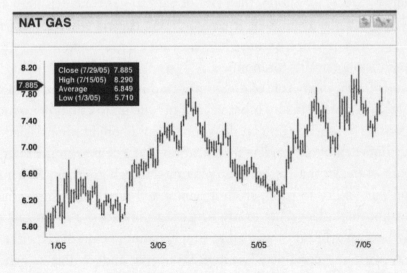

Figure I.1: Natural Gas, January–August 2005 (traded between $6 and $8)

(see figure I.2). When there is an actual, physical supply disruption, it takes many months for that market to return to normal. You can't build a new refinery or repair a damaged one overnight. That was how we knew that we would have a favorable trading opportunity for many months to come.

When I look back, how I worked with my traders during that fateful week remains one of the highlights of my career. We went on to have a record September, October, November, and December. That was because of the restraint we showed before the advent of the storm and how we used the capital that we had preserved to make a killing in the lengthy bull market in natural gas that resulted from Katrina. It was as if the entire structure of the natural gas market had been altered and put on a multimonth tear after the storm.

What happened to the price of natural gas the day the storm hit set the tone for the natural gas market for the rest of the year (see figure I.2). The storm made landfall in southeast Louisiana on August 29, 2005. On that day alone, the price of natural gas opened at $11.95, traded as high as $12.07, and closed at $10.84. However, that was only the start of the great bull market in natural gas. In fact, by December 2005, the price of natural gas traded as high as $15.78. That is the kind of price action that traders yearn for, often for months or years, because it creates such a great opportunity to rack up huge profits for months.

In 2005, in my role of director of trading, I made more money than I ever made in any other year of my life up to that point. And it was all because during Guilt Week I focused on limiting risk and putting each of our traders in a position to participate in the aftermath of the storm. Rather than playing a hunch going in, Katrina and our ability to profit from it hammered home an insight that has become a key tenet in my investing philosophy: never make big bets on arbitrary events that simply cannot be predicted either way with any certainty. Compulsive people and gamblers spend their money on hunches and make arbitrary bets. They let their

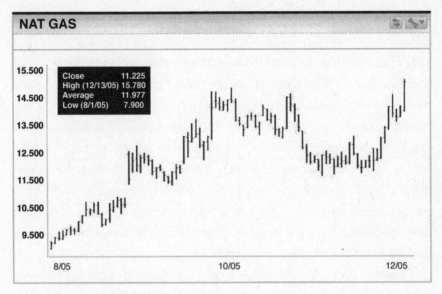

Figure I.2: Natural Gas, August–December 2005 (traded from $8 to $16)

emotions get the best of them. Savvy traders and investors manage risk, monitor the market, and put themselves in positions to succeed. This idea may sound obvious, but if you think about some of your investing decisions—and you're honest with yourself—you'll probably be forced to admit that you've been gambling when you thought you were investing.

My colleagues and I celebrated a very profitable 2005 with the ultimate holiday party. We rented out the nightclub Crobar and spent many hundreds of thousands of dollars on a party that I'll never forget. We had such a great year that we were able to hire three pop stars that night: Reina, Rihanna, and LL Cool J. Things just didn't get better than that in the trading game.

Katrina turned out to be a classic case of buying high and selling higher. After the storm hit the price of natural gas soared, hitting a new 52-week high (as shown in Figure I.2). MBF's traders still had a large window that allowed them to trade natural gas for months and make money along the way. That is the best way to make money in any market: identifying those rare opportunities in which one identifies assets that can break out and deliver outsized returns.

The way that the best professional traders were thinking about markets during the Katrina catastrophe holds lessons for today's individual investors. Why? Because in the ensuing five years, individual investors have seen even the safest precincts of the stock market experience the kind of volatility that once were reserved for commodities. For better or worse, we're all traders now. And even if Vanguard's John Bogle or Charles Schwab is tucking your ultra-conservative portfolio into bed at night, you need to understand that the markets are irreparably changed and that relying solely on the old rules is a recipe for disaster.

Lastly, there is one more important reason why investment professionals view the market differently in 2011 than we did pre-Katrina. Since the Great Recession and the fall of Lehman Brothers in September 2008, it hasn't only been volatility in equities and commodities that has surged. The other important change is that uncertainty has surged as well. The new normal is characterized by fear and uncertainty, and not just for retail investors. New times demand new tactics: welcome to buying high and selling higher.

Before I introduce you to the new model, I don't expect you to take me on my word that the classic investing strategy—known as buy-and-hold investing—is broken. So let's look at the data. A buy-and-hold strategy might have been a solid investment tactic during the last great bull market (1982–2000), but no longer. If buy-and-hold investing still worked, then an investor would have been able to buy an S&P Index Fund in 2000, put it in his or her portfolio, and ride it like an escalator until 2010. That's not the case. The S&P was down roughly 10 percent in the past decade.

To drive home the point further, let's look at the vaunted company Microsoft, which was a growth stock from 1981 to 2001. It traded as high as $59 per share in 2000. However, within a year that stock, once considered a great growth stock, traded in the $20–$30 range. But buying Microsoft in 2000 would have been a mistake, since it has not exceeded $40 since then and in early 2011 still traded at less than $30 per share.

Buying Microsoft (MSFT) at any time after 2001 and holding it would have been a losing proposition in the "New Normal" (see figure I.3). A $10,000 investment in MSFT in early 2000 would be worth less than $5,000 today. I would much prefer stocks and commodities that have outperformed the averages and its peers than those that have fared far worse.

Microsoft is just one of many companies that struggled during the first decade of the new millennium. Many have called this decade the Lost Decade, a similar phenomenon to what Japan's markets experienced in the 1980s and 1990s. Japan is in much worse shape, though, as its markets are still off 75 percent from their 1989 high. I do not consider the last decade as the Lost Decade. To me it was the Decade of the Emerging Market (see chapter 2).

If investors should no longer buy and hold blue chips like Microsoft, then what should they do? Investors need to change their mind-set. They must become more tactical in their investments.

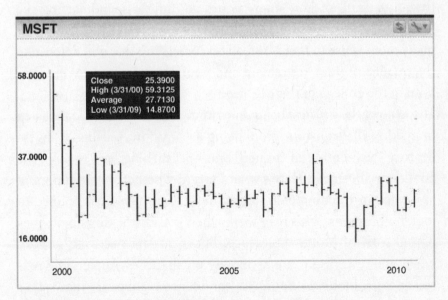

Figure I.3: 10-Year Chart of MSFT, January 2000–March 2011

Individual investors need to be more active in managing their own money. They must learn to think more like traders, but with this caveat: do not day-trade. I do not recommend trading every day or even every week. That is a losing proposition. However, sticking one's head in the sand by ignoring quarterly statements from your stockbroker—which many "experts" recommend—is an even worse proposition.

This does not mean selling and buying stocks every week or two just to generate activity. It means selling or building up a particular holding (also known as "trading around positions") and shifting allocations six to eight times a year. We're active managers of every other aspect of our lives, so why would we not be active managers in terms of wealth creation?

If you put more time into researching the purchase of your new car or a major appliance than you did your last stock trade, then you may need to step up your due diligence if you want to thrive in today's markets. This means spending more time each week researching macro trends, the stock market, and individual stocks. If you are wondering where you will find the time to do that, just think of how many hours you might spend surfing the Net each week or the time you lose watching television. Doesn't it make more sense to focus instead on something that will determine the quality of your retirement and your ability to send your children to the college of their choice?

One of the greatest epiphanies in my career—and the first step in making the transition from being a "buy-low, sell-high" investor to a "buy-high, sell-higher" one—is learning how to be in the confidence business. Here's what I mean: whether we are shopping at Costco or tracking tech stocks, most of us have been trained to look for bargains. This may work when you're stocking up on five-pound tubs of Motts applesauce, but it doesn't necessarily work when you're trying to make money on shares of Apple. The reason it is profitable to be in the confidence business is that rather than buying stocks that are making new lows (or, as I like to call it, the "catching falling knives" business), the confidence business is all about buying stocks that the market likes: stocks with momentum, stocks that are outperforming the average benchmark indexes like the S&P 500, and, more specifically, stocks that are outperforming other stocks in the same sector. Both measures are the essence of *relative outperformance*. (Relative outperformance is comparing an asset's performance to a different asset or index.) This method of selecting stocks is superior to trying to buy stocks on the cheap. When we buy low and sell high, we're really just buying stocks that appear to be bargains but really are sucker bets because momentum—and the majority of investors and traders— is going against them.

This idea of buying high and selling higher goes against the basic principle of value investing—one of the most touted methods of investing for decades. Like buy-and hold investing, the typical model of value investing also is broken (value investing is simply buying securities that are priced lower than their intrinsic value). In today's volatile markets, it is often the value stock that turns into a rapidly devaluing one when the markets start to roll over. In contrast to Microsoft, an investor could have bought the innovative company 3M in 2000 and fared far better than if he had bought Microsoft. At the beginning of 1995, 3M was trading at around $29 per share. In late 2000, 3M exceeded $60 per share before closing that year near $50. So, although 3M was not cheap, it was still a good value because it was a rising star. Buying 3M at any time between $50 and $60 would have been a smart buy, even though the stock was up significantly over the prior five years. In July 2007, at the height of the market, 3M hit an all-time high of just under $96 per share.

However, investors could not have simply bought that stock and tucked it away for their retirement. That's because the liquidity crisis of 2008–09 caused 3M to drop all the way down to the low $40s in March 2009. The price movement of 3M shows why buy-and-hold is no longer a viable investing model (see figure I.4).

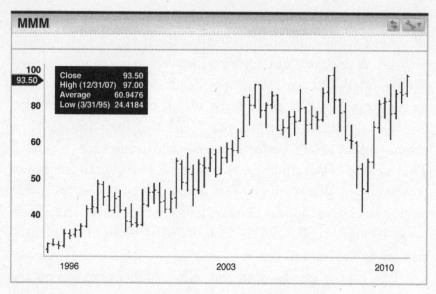

Figure I.4: 15-Year Chart of 3M, January 1995–March 2011

Buying high and selling higher is a much better technique than buying low and hoping that the stock you just bought for cheap—a stock that may be in a tailspin—will somehow turn around and deliver big profits.

I realize these are pretty bold claims, and hindsight is 20/20. After all, who am I to say that the tried-and-true philosophies of buy-and-hold investing and value investing are flawed? I am not an academic like Benjamin Graham and David Dodd were when the Wall Street Crash of 1929 prompted them to come up with a new, safe investing method. The result of their research, *Security Analysis*, became the bible of value investing, the sacred text for many of today's leading investors, including Warren Buffett.

I am not a PhD. I'm just a regular guy who is in the markets every day, observing, learning, and honing my discipline. And *Buy High, Sell Higher* is my response to the series of jaw-dropping events that I have witnessed in the markets in recent years—events that have made me realize that the average investor needs a new plan if he is going to survive and profit in a market that Graham and Dodd would barely recognize. And I believe that anyone who is prepared to do his homework and be prepared for the unexpected can become a better investor if he willingly embraces the concept of buying high and selling higher.

Of course, no one wins in the markets all the time, and I am by no means an investor with a perfect track record. I have made some boneheaded mistakes—plenty of them. I have held stocks far too long and sold them far too soon. I've taken on excessive risk. But I like to think that I have matured and evolved as an investor during the past few years. Discipline has been my top priority and it has turned me into a much more effective investor.

I've also taken the time to figure out what I'm good at—and what I'm not. I was a failure as a pit trader. In fact, it makes perfect sense that I would fail at pit trading. I am by nature an introvert, and the best pit traders are outgoing, gregarious people who have no fear of trading in such a public, crowded arena. But even if I were outgoing and gregarious, that would not have been a game changer. I also lacked the necessary discipline to be a successful pit trader. But today I enjoy success because I practice all of the advice I've learned working shoulder to shoulder with great traders like my mentor, Mark Fisher. Fisher was—and still is—an incredible trader because he lived the edict of protecting the downside first. Fisher also taught me the importance of doing my homework.

Finally, if there is a lesson to be taken away from the way MBF avoided the fate of Amaranth and ended up having a banner year after Hurricane Katrina, it is to be ready for the unexpected. I have learned that the unexpected can have a profound effect on a particular stock or on the market as a whole. For example, in his wildest dreams, President Barack Obama would never have predicted that there would be an ecological disaster in the Gulf of Mexico during his second year in the White House. If he had been asked at his inauguration for the ten things he was most worried about occurring during his presidency, the BP disaster would never have made the list. The same thing would have been true if in 2006 you had asked Lehman Brothers CEO Richard Fuld about what would eventually bring his 158-year-old investment bank crashing down in the fall of 2008.

If these major unexpected events have taught us anything, it is that anything is possible, and investors need to understand and embrace that reality. Having a rainy-day fund is one of the greatest tools in the investors' arsenals. It affords them the opportunity to buy high and sell higher when these once-in-a-blue-moon opportunities come up.

# PART I

# THINK LIKE A PROFESSIONAL

# Buy High, Sell Higher

One of the realities of investing is that it is much easier to get into the market than to get out of it. In fact, there are no barriers to entry into the stock market. Anyone with a stockbroker or an online brokerage account can buy a stock and make a case for why it is worth buying now.

It is far more difficult to figure out when to sell a stock or exit a position, particularly if you are facing a potential loss. Selling a stock that you have held for years at a loss is an admission of failure, and few among us like to admit failure.

It also is difficult for most investors to buy a stock after it has run up, say, five or ten points in the span of a few days or weeks. They feel that they missed their best chance to buy into that stock. Similarly, most investors do not want to buy stocks after they have hit a 52-week high. These are some of the reasons why so many retail investors fail. They have the wrong mind-set going in.

If you are going to buy high and sell higher, you'll need to understand how to pick your point of entry for each investment. In this chapter, we'll look at what it means to buy confidence, as well as how to come up with your own "buy signs" by using some basic fundamental and technical analysis. Fundamental analysis is more of a snapshot of a security at a given point in time. Three classic books I would recommend on these topics are Jesse Livermore's *Reminiscences of a Stock Operator* (for fundamental analysis), John Murphy's *Technical Analysis of the Financial Markets*, and Jack Schwager's *Market Wizards*. I'll also show you how to look at moving averages and trading volume to determine when to get into the market. It may sound like a lot of heavy lifting, but if you can spot patterns in other aspects of your life, you'll be able to do it with the market.

## Buying High Means Buying Confidence

The stock market has a way of scaring some people away from stocks that have momentum—which might be heading higher. On the other hand, the inability to understand downward momentum sometimes makes people stay with other investments—losing investments that are headed lower—far longer than they should.

As investors, we're always asking, "What if?" *What if I get out and the stock goes higher and higher?* But this is where we go wrong. I have heard many so-called experts say that the key to trading is to buy low and sell high. I couldn't disagree more. The key to investing is to buy high but sell even higher. That's what trading and investing are really all about.

When you buy low and sell high, you might be right four out of five times—if you are really lucky. However, it's the fifth time, that one time out of five, when you buy a stock that really tanks, when you lose all of your gains plus some. That's why I urge investors to stay away from the "buy low, sell high" strategy.

When you buy high, you are buying confidence. You are buying a security in which there is conviction surrounding that stock and its price. People are paying that premium, a higher price, which is what makes this strategy far more reliable than the alternative. And confidence has a way of feeding on itself—attracting more and more buyers to that particular security, propelling the stock ever higher.

There is one more critical reason for eschewing the falling-knife method of investing. When you buy a stock that is consistently making new lows or has just made a 52-week low, you have no point of reference to tell you what to do with that stock (i.e., when to sell or reduce your position). When I say there are no reference points when buying falling knives, I mean that many investors lack the ability to identify that stock's risk, to quantify or calculate its risk, or to find a price point where risk can be established. Put another way, once an asset has fallen through its 52-week low, no investor, professional or otherwise, has any idea on how much farther that security can fall. As a result, investors have no idea when to sell or reduce their holdings.

## Analyzing Your Investments

For those who have limited knowledge on what to look for when analyzing a stock, don't worry. In my experience, only a small percentage of retail investors know what to look for when evaluating different kinds of opportunities. It is through technical analysis and fundamental analysis that stock market pros analyze a particular security. While this is not a book on either (there are plenty of good books and websites devoted to both), it is important to mention them here so that you will know how to conduct further research on these methods of analysis, and have at least a working knowledge of them so that the examples I use in the book are readily understandable.

I have been surprised that so many individual investors who hold stocks have less of a working knowledge of either type of analysis—something I also have heard from many money and wealth managers who work with affluent investors. This information is so vital that I suggest you start here but do additional research on your own. Throughout the book I will be discussing specific securities and how they are faring when measured against certain key indicators, such as a "moving average." As someone who aspires to buy high and sell higher, I have found that technical analysis (a method of analyzing a security based on data, statistics, and patterns) is a more useful method of analyzing stocks than fundamental analysis (a method of analyzing a security based on its financials, operations, and prospects). Here are a few words about each.

Moving averages, which are no more than the average price of an asset over a certain period of time, are used by experienced market professionals to identify future trends based on past performance.* Conducting this type of analysis comes under the heading of technical analysis, which uses charts to help predict the future price of a security.

When you buy a stock that is making new highs (as opposed to new lows), you have several points of reference, such as the 50-day, 100-day, and 200-day moving averages. You can find all three of these moving averages in minutes for any security on hundreds of free sites like Yahoo! Finance (finance.yahoo.com).

All three of these reference points (50-day, 100-day, and 200-day) are used as important indicators of strength and confidence. When buying higher—buying confidence—sometimes there are so many points of reference that it can become difficult to pick which one to use. Because it is perceived to be the most reliable

---

*If you have no experience with researching moving averages, I think it is important to give an example of how to locate those before we go further. Let's stick with the free site Yahoo! Finance, since they make it easy to locate these indicators. Once you get to the home page, next to "get quotes" type in the ticker symbol "IBM." Once that is done, then locate "1y" (one year) under the chart and click that. Now you have a one-year chart of IBM. Lastly, locate the "Technical Indicators" button above the chart and click on "Simple Moving Average" on the drop-down menu. Three slots come up. The first one already has "50-day" in the top box called "Line 1 Period." Type in "100" and "200" in the other two boxes, and you will now have a one-year chart of IBM and the three most relevant averages, the 50-, 100-, and 200-day moving averages. In late 2010, IBM can be seen as breaking out above all three of those averages, indicating the strength of the stock.

over the longest period of time, the 200-day moving average is the one most used by most market professionals. I use it as my top indicator, and I recommend that you stick to that one as your chief indicator of strength. When a stock falls through that key benchmark, you are likely to see the stock sell off because that is what the pros are looking at. And you want to be among the first to get out—not the last.

However, sometimes an asset is moving so quickly that a 200-day moving average is simply too long a period to be of much help to an investor. In some cases, you must tighten your indicators and shorten your duration period of analysis. By way of example here, we'll look at commodities, which generally are much more volatile than stocks and, therefore, are better examples for our purposes. Volatility in equities generally spikes in down markets. Because of that, a stock that is sliding isn't going to break the 200-day moving average. However, using a 50-day moving average as a reference point for stocks might be more useful.

For example, Apple (APPL) fell below the 50-day moving average during the credit crisis of September 2008. In early 2009, Apple began to challenge the 50-day moving average. By that, I mean that Apple was trying to break above that reference point and it did. That moment was the precursor to Apple's confidence story. By April 2009, Apple started to build, and it never fell below the 200-day moving average again. So the 50-day moving average proved to be a very useful Mason-Dixon Line for determining when to trim and when to add to a position in Apple.

In very volatile periods, it is better to use a 50-day moving average as a reference point rather than a 200-day moving average. This is especially true for commodities. For example, in 2008, when oil was racing to $147 per barrel (up from $20 a barrel a few years earlier), a 200-day average simply would not work in helping you to figure out the direction of the price of oil. In that case, I used a maximum 50-day moving average to figure out when to pare down my holdings. Anything greater than a 50-day would not be helpful in telling me what I needed to know about the future direction of that stock.

You need to use common sense in figuring out which moving average to use. However, 80 percent of the time, a 200-day moving average will serve you well, but if an asset seems to be moving at 100 miles per hour when the rest of the market is going at about 40, then that is a situation that calls for you to tighten up the indicators as outlined above.

Another way that market professionals analyze stocks comes under the heading of fundamental analysis (as opposed to technical analysis). Fundamental analysis uses financial statements and other qualitative and quantitative data to measure a security's value at a particular point in time. For example, when an expert says that Exxon Mobil (XOM) has a strong "balance sheet" because it has so much cash on hand, she is telling investors that this is a company in strong financial health. (A balance sheet measure a firm's assets, liabilities, and shareholder equity.) This is a textbook example of fundamental analysis.

Fundamental analysis also can include macro issues such as the overall growth prospects of an industry or the economy as a whole, but most traders use fundamental analysis to look at company-specific criteria such as earnings, future growth prospects, and anything else that might help a company achieve some sort of sustainable competitive advantage. For example, when you hear someone say that a stock is trading at a P/E ratio of 5, that means that the stock has a current share price (P) of $10 and earnings per share (E) of $2 ($10 \div 2 = 5$). Companies with high P/E ratios generally are considered more risky than those with lower ratios.

## How "Buy High, Sell Higher" Works: Continental Airlines

Buying high and selling higher involves a process. To teach you how the process works, I want to use an actual example of an investing opportunity I didn't catch quickly enough. In order to give you more insight into what I look for in a stock, we are going to look back at a specific opportunity that provided investors a large window in which to get in. I kick myself on this one, because it was right there in clear sight and I missed it.

It starts with the assumptions I held in late 2009. Going into 2010, I looked at the airline industry, and rather than strength I saw vulnerability. I figured with the slowdown in consumer spending, people would be cutting back, which would have an adverse effect on the airlines. However, there were clearly identifiable signs that Continental (CAL) was a stock to buy and it was an easy trade to follow, both by doing some fundamental analysis (e.g., strong earnings, increased capacity) and technical analysis (the price of the stock was signaling a buy). Let's take a closer look at both.

Fundamentally, tremendous shifts had occurred in Continental Airlines' business plan, which I will discuss in a moment. Other airlines also made some meaningful changes to their businesses, but they did not move as quickly as CAL, so they were not as attractive.

Following the credit crisis of 2008, there was no shortage of rumors that the airline industry was going to be the next to be nationalized (like the financial giants Fannie Mae and Freddie Mac) or bailed out like the auto industry. However, there was absolutely no truth to those rumors.

In fact, the reality was the management of the airline industry did a better job than any other industry in the United States of changing and adapting quickly to the great recession of 2008–09. They managed the bottom line phenomenally, cut back costs, and introduced secondary fees—fees that consumers had never been accustomed to previously: bag fees, seat fees, extra-leg-room fees. They began to charge for things like food and eventually even for blankets. In the process of making those changes, airlines reduced capacity, making them more efficient businesses. All of these factors helped the fundamentals of the company.

In essence, by making the changes they did, even though

consumers hated the changes, most airlines improved upon their business model in a significant way. They were now getting revenue for things like standby fees and other things that would have been unthinkable only a year or two earlier. They adapted their model so that their businesses could make money in the slow-growth environment that existed in 2009.

Now let's see how the stock performed against the backdrop I just described. In early January 2009, Continental traded as high as $21.83. During the first quarter of 2009, which I like to call "the winter of our discontent," Continental sold off to a low on March 9, an "Armageddon" low of $6.37. The stock was down a stunning 75 percent from its most recent high (see figure 1.1).

Continental spent the remainder of the year recovering and got as high as $17.65 on October 15, 2009, about six weeks before Thanksgiving. The key is to determine when to get into that stock in order to buy it high and sell it higher. From a technical basis (that is, from how it looked on the charts when compared to key

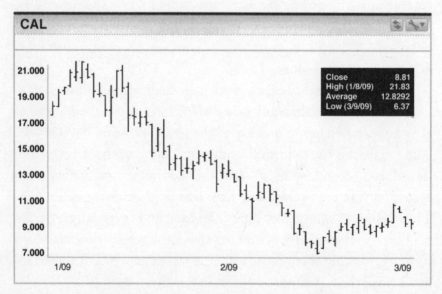

Figure 1.1: Continental (CAL) Stock Chart, January 1, 2009–March 31, 2009

moving average indicators), the window started to open at the end of November.

I do not like to trade on Mondays ("Turnaround Tuesdays" have a way of reversing Monday's action, making Monday's trade a fool's bet). After a weekend, and especially after a holiday weekend, traders often have had a tough few days with their kids and in-laws, and they come in Monday looking to blow off some steam. That often has the effect of a market that is trading not on fundamentals but on emotion. I'd much rather digest the information and make my decision the next day. Monday, November 30, the first day back after the Thanksgiving holiday, was no exception.

After Continental made a high of $17.65 on October 15, it retreated through the end of October into early November and gave investors no indication or signal technically that it should be a buy (see figure 1.2).

On November 30, the stock opened at $13.54. It proceeded to rally throughout the day, up to $14.30. It closed at $14.26. Why

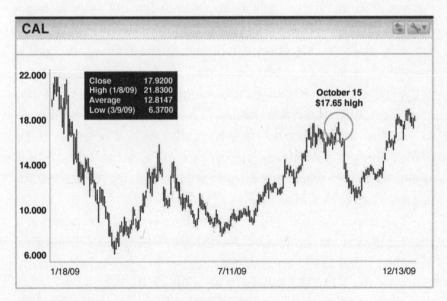

Figure 1.2: CAL, January–December 2009

was I following the price of the stock so closely? Because that close came within six cents of a return north of the 50-day moving average, which was at $14.32. If it had settled at $14.33, it would have been above the 50-, 100-, and 200-day moving averages, which, as I stated before, is a very strong sign of strength. In addition, the 30-day average volume had not exceeded the average 30-day volume since November 9. But November 30 was a day that we identify as the *beginning* of a potential opportunity.

The key day was the next day, Tuesday—Turnaround Tuesday—the first day one should have looked at *possibly* getting into that stock. On Tuesday, December 1, CAL closed above the 50-, 100-, and 200-day moving averages for the first time since January 2009. However, there was one bearish signal as well, which investors needed to take into account: the 30-day volume. Although the volume rose that day, it did not exceed the average 30-day average volume. That is important. Volume tells you the rest of the "buy high, sell higher" story. That's because it is another strong indicator of a stock's strength. Weak volume indicates that a stock is lacking in confidence—that the confidence story has not yet built up. It also tells a supply-and-demand story because demand for a specific equity is measured in terms of volume, particularly in the acceleration of volume. If the moving average is the speedometer on a professional trader's dashboard, the volume is the RPM gauge. Although the volume rose that day, it did not exceed the 30-day average volume. The horsepower wasn't there.

At that point, I would have correctly advised investors to be patient and not pull the trigger on this stock at this point. Once again, that was because the 30-day volume did not reinforce buying into that stock at that time.

The important thing to recognize here is that I was building a case for buying the stock. On December 1, which was Turnaround Tuesday, I had CAL on my radar screen as a stock I potentially wanted to own. On Wednesday, December 2, the volume exceeded the average 30-day volume for the first time since November 9.

The stock did 9.35 million shares, and the average 30-day volume was 7.84 million. The higher-than-average 30-day volume, along with the fact that the stock continued to trade above the 50-, 100-, and 200-day moving averages, formed a definite buy sign. This is a stock I should have bought going into the close, which was $15.67 on December 2.

Indicators were aligned. Volume was strong. With two closes above the 200-day moving average, a buy sign was present. I should have been in that trade at $15.67. However, this was such a solid opportunity that it offered future points to get in.

In the ensuing days and weeks, an investor could have bought the stock and put in a 3 percent stop loss order on it, which is 47 cents. A 3 percent decline from $15.67 (47 cents) puts the stop loss order at $15.20. The key is that had you bought the stock then and put in that stop loss order, you would never have been stopped out. (A stop loss order is an order placed by an investor to automatically sell that security when it falls to or below a predetermined level.) Since hitting that price of $15.67, CAL never traded at $15.20 or below. This was shaping up to be a pretty remarkable opportunity. Here it was late 2009, and the stock remained well north of where I should have bought it.

Not only did I miss the trade, I tried to "fade the trade," meaning shorting the stock, and I lost money (fading, or shorting, a stock is when an investor tries to profit on the falling price of a particular asset). Why did I get it so wrong?

I stumbled on this one so badly because I had such a negative view of the airline industry going in. I tried to sell the airlines short in February 2009. Looking back, I realized what I had missed. When I rolled up my sleeves and really looked at it, I saw this as an example of a tremendous opportunity. That's because the actual risk on buying CAL when all the stars aligned was only 3 percent, which seems incredible. But that's all it was—the downside of this trade was 3 percent.

For the record, I personally don't like to buy a stock and say,

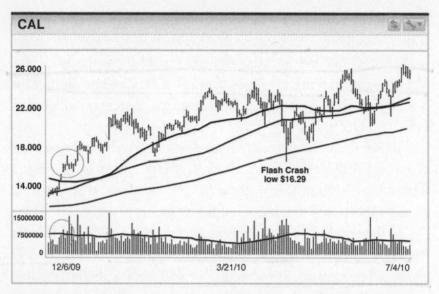

Figure 1.3: CAL Daily Chart Nov. 20, 2009 to July 31, 2010. The early December 2009 trade is circled. The 30-day volume average is shown on the bottom with early December again circled. The chart also includes 50-, 100-, 200-day moving averages, and finally a note under Flash Crash low of $16.29.

"I am going to risk 3 percent" and then put a stop loss order in at that point. Instead, I like to find a point of reference. I identify something that I can see either technically or fundamentally on a given asset and work with that. I might look for the stock to fall through its 50-, 100-, or 200-day moving average. Or I might see volume start to fall. Or I will use a time stop. That is, if I don't get the results I am looking for in, say, three months, I will sell that security. In many cases, if I have done all the right prep work, that stock or commodity should not violate the 3 percent stop in any event. When I get it right, I guarantee that in every instance, both of those conditions—a point-of-reference stop or a time stop— will never exceed the 3 percent. I like to keep a very tight leash on the stocks that I buy because, like the best of investors, I am always monitoring the downside. Investors who say that 3 percent seems like a very narrow range are correct. But remember, the key is to keep your losses to an absolute minimum those times when you are wrong so that when you get it right, you can be sure that your gains are greater than your losses.

*[handwritten notes]* 2 days - $400 loss on 200 shares or 3 months - which ever comes first ✓

## You Don't Have to Be the First One In

You might be asking how to time the market so effectively. After all, you probably have a full-time job and don't have eighty hours a week to devote to watching your stocks and the financial markets. However, you don't need to be a market genius to get in on the Continental Airlines trade we just discussed. Say, like me, you missed the CAL play in fall 2009. Going forward, the market almost always gives you a second chance to get back in. You had a sell-off that provided you another chance to buy into the stock. When was that? It was during the Flash Crash of 2010.

On May 6, 2010, the Dow roiled as investors worried about the debt crisis that was sending Greece into a political and economic frenzy. During the day, the Dow lost 900 points—and recovered them within a matter of minutes. It was the second-largest intraday point swing (1,010.14 points) and the biggest one-day decline (998.5 points) in the Dow's history. On October 10, 2008, the Dow had the largest intraday trading range of 1,018.77 points. The Flash Crash made all the headlines the next day. What made it so noteworthy was that the entire market dropped so quickly and that no one could figure out why it happened.

Investors who had not only a disciplined system in place but a clear investing strategy and a written investment plan could have weathered the Flash Crash much better than those who didn't.

The Flash Crash is something to really think about, because you're probably going to say this doesn't make sense. I want you to think about something. As powerful as that Flash Crash was, it even respected the 3 percent down rule on Continental Airlines, meaning even a thousand-point drop in the Dow did not cause investors to get out of the stock.

Let's summarize: We identified December 2 as the moment to flip the switch on Continental Airlines. Why? We finally got volume back above the 30-day average volume. We also were above the 50-, 100-, and 200-day moving averages; we've had a second consecutive settlement (closes) above that. I like to use two consecutive closes above all three of those moving averages, and that was the first time that happened since January. $15.20 was the line in the sand, the point that an investor holding the stock should have been out of the trade.

The other real key here is that the price of the stock continued to rise. You didn't have to get in those first days of December. The window of opportunity stayed open for months to come. You could have bought that stock at any point along the way. It never got below $15.20. It proceeded to rise until April 15, 2010, to $24.29, an increase of 55 percent from the first entry point of $15.67. You do not have to be a trader to cash in on this stock. This was such a great investment that you could have bought that stock and held it for a year and still made money.

There is one more interesting wrinkle to the Continental Airlines story worth noting. On the same day I indicated that the stock was beginning to become a buy—December 1—Goldman Sachs downgraded Continental's debt. This is usually perceived to be a negative, and might make many investors avoid the stock. However, this was a case of debt being downgraded and the market just shrugging it off. The stock did not react negatively to the news. It is important to note that downgrading the company's debt is not the same thing as downgrading the stock. A debt downgrade should be perceived as far more onerous and a structural change for the company's balance sheet and earnings growth potential. Downgrading the stock is cyclical and can be quickly reversed with a favorable revision higher.

The last concept I want to discuss here is "maximize winners, minimize losers." What does that mean, exactly? In essence, it's one of the things I think investors don't do enough. It's about setting priorities: first, protect the downside and recognize that when you have a winning stock, you need to stay with it and not sell it too early (you want to maximize the amount of your gains). Most people, when they have a profit, like to immediately sell the stock and ring the cash register. The key is recognizing how to stay with your winners. Most people take their profits way too soon. That's one of the key issues that I've found in dealing with other traders. In subsequent chapters, I will show you what to look for so that you can maximize your winners and reap greater profits from your best investments.

# 2

# Strategize First, Trade Second

One of the greatest mistakes investors make is trading first and rationalizing the trade later. If I asked a hundred investors how many of them have a written investing plan in place, I am confident that at least seventy-five would have to admit they didn't.

In this chapter, I'll show you where to get your investing ideas and how to transform them into buying opportunities. You'll also understand how macro forces like the global economy, commodity prices, and what the Federal Reserve is up to can help or hinder your ideas. Finally, I will summarize one of my recent investment plans so that you can see how these elements all come together to form an investing strategy.

The first thing every investor needs to do is to devise a strategy. Every investor needs to have a plan that's tangible, that's written, and that can be referred back to whenever necessary. Only with such a plan can you look back and say, "Here's what I said. Here's where I want to be."

One of the greatest professional football coaches of all time, Bill Walsh of the San Francisco 49ers, always had the first twenty to twenty-five plays scripted before his team ever took the field.

That's one of the reasons Walsh's team won six division titles, three NFC Championship titles, and three Super Bowls.

People who watch shows like CNBC's *Fast Money* (a show of which I am one of the hosts) probably think that all of the things we discuss are things we know intuitively or can rattle off because we are stock market sages. That's nowhere near the truth. Although I have learned a great deal about the financial markets over the years, I still spend at least a couple of hours every day reading company reports and filings and other pertinent documents (such as a company's 10K, which is like an annual report but includes more in-depth data on the firm's financials, management team, and so forth), not to mention watching the overall market action as well as the price movements of particular stocks, other investments, and potential investments.

I mean no disrespect by this, but I think that most investors are lazy. Many love the rush of trading, but few want to put in the time and effort necessary to become more effective investors.

Whatever the amount of time you devote to investing, at least 90 percent should be spent doing research, monitoring the market environment, and developing a strategic investment plan. One of the best places to start a plan is with allocation: How much money are you going to devote to the market this year? Where, when, and how are you going to deploy your capital? But before you start thinking about how much you want to invest or what kind of profits you're looking for, you need to think about what's at stake.

## Set Salary Caps for Your Investments and Your Portfolio

Sports has a concept called the salary cap. The salary cap sets the maximum amount of money a sports team can pay its entire roster of players as well as how much a team can spend for each of its individual players. Similarly, I like to think of myself as the general manager of my own investments, complete with salary caps for my entire portfolio as well as for individual investments.

So, for part of my investing plan, at the beginning of each year, I set a maximum amount of money that I will allocate to the markets that year, as well as a minimum amount. For example, I might decide to allocate no more than $100,000 to the market in the upcoming year and no less than $50,000. The actual maximum and minimum amounts matter less than setting that overall investing salary cap for the entire portfolio.

I also set a salary cap for each investment. This helps to ensure that I am at least minimally diversified in my portfolio. I make sure that no more than one third of the value of my total portfolio is devoted to any one sector, such as energy or technology. The maximum amount that I allocate to any one "player" (i.e., investment) in any one year is 12 percent of the total investment. I insert a time element to each player/investment when establishing my salary caps, and I evaluate all my investments on a quarterly or monthly basis.

I also set a limit to the total number of players that I can have on my team at any one time. I set that number at a minimum of nine players and a maximum of twenty-two players. You may ask how I came up with twenty-two. I believe in the consistency of numbers, and I have found that this number has worked very well for me. Any more than twenty-two stocks make it difficult to manage that portfolio.

Bringing the salary cap concept to your investments also allows you to maintain position flexibility, since you are consistently paring down or selling positions (i.e., players), and that helps you to have cash in hand when an attractive opportunity comes along. We'll talk more about position flexibility in chapter 7, but suffice to say here that maintaining position flexibility means leaving yourself in a position to take advantage of the one or two market anomalies per year that present themselves as investing opportunities. It's not just about having the cash or resources on hand to make these investments; it's also about not placing yourself in a position where you are holding nonperforming assets that tie up your capital.

The reality is that in most asset classes, only three or four buy signs pop up during the course of the year. (These changes in the prices of individual stocks are different from the opportunities that come along every few years.) The Continental Airlines example from the previous chapter is one of those rare opportunities. Again, you need position flexibility. Having a salary cap in place helps bring flexibility to your investing plan so you can be ready when opportunities come along.

## Pick Your Asset Classes

A salary cap is just the beginning. Every investor has to craft his or her own strategic plan, including which asset classes to be invested in during the course of the year (e.g., stocks, bonds, cash), how to be allocated, where and when to get into the market, where and when to get out, and how long to give each investment to pan out. However, the key is to start with a macro picture of the entire investment arena.

Before you can select specific stocks and sectors, you have to determine if this is going to be a positive year for equities, and if so, which sectors or areas you will focus on. You may decide instead that commodities may be the better investment theme (for more on commodities, see chapter 9). This decision-making process is one in which you need to measure the potential for corporations to expand margins and earnings per share. You have to measure supply and demand. You have to measure the global demand for natural resources. You have to understand the potential trajectory for interest rates and currencies. Once you have researched these areas, you will have a better sense of whether to focus on stocks, commodities, or other assets. Once the macro plan is written, then you can focus on developing a list of potential, specific assets and securities that you want to watch and buy.

Creating such a plan will force you to be more cognizant of each asset in your portfolio. For example, you may have a stock that you have held in your portfolio for eighteen months even though it has dropped by 30 percent. Some experts will call that a long-term investment. That's ridiculous. That's not a long-term investment; that's a *bad* investment. We've reached a point now where we clearly need to identify it as such. Your investment plan can help you recognize which investments you should buy or sell—or hold—depending on how they are helping you reach your investing goals. And although your written plan is a guide, it also can be a little fluid. Each year, I make a plan, I write it down, and I update my thinking quarterly and also make adjustments monthly. I will show investors how they need to attack this critical task later in this chapter.

## Where to Get Your Investing Ideas

Professional traders know that doing their homework—their due diligence—is crucial to successful investing. As mentioned, a good 90 percent of your time should be spent researching and preparing to invest. Part of that means you should be investigating potential investments.

People often ask me what they should be reading to make sure they are staying abreast of the markets, macro trends, and more targeted information as well as what sectors to invest in and what stocks to buy. This is a key question, and the good news is that with the advent of the Internet, there are scores of places to turn to in order to get up to speed on essential topics that will shape your investment plan.

Reading publications and accessing social websites is only the beginning of your search for investing information. In recent years, many investment banking firms, such as Merrill Lynch and Morgan Stanley, have vastly increased the amount of educational resources they make available to their clients. One very helpful addition has been videotaped roundtable discussions of investment professionals. I have found these roundtables to be immensely helpful (and you often can watch these on the web via investment company websites).

In fact, I also have hosted roundtables over the years. Seated around me are portfolio managers who are experts in different asset classes. I also listen in on investing roundtables and find that I always come away with at least a new idea or two that was not on my radar screen before the event. I do the same thing when I appear on *Fast Money*. When fellow panelists Karen Finerman, Tim Seymour, Pete Najarian, and Guy Adami mention a trend, a stock, or an investing idea that I have not thought of, I write it down so I can research it and possibly act on it later.

There are many other useful educational opportunities available through brokers and other financial sites. For example, online brokerage firms like TD Ameritrade (www.tdameritrade.com) and Fidelity (www.fidelity.com) offer a great many opportunities for investors to gain access to financial experts who can widen their view of the markets. They offer these via their own websites or link up with other educational firms that offer a plethora of investing webcasts, courses, market and trading discussions, etc.

Some educational events are more macro-oriented, looking at different global markets, while others are so micro-oriented as to recommend specific stocks. The key is to avail yourself of the resources that your broker's site or other sites offer, almost always for free, to clients.

## Constructing Your Plan

In order to put together a coherent investing plan, you want to make sure that you have put in the time and research so that you have a sense of where you want to invest in the year ahead.

I write a comprehensive investing plan once a quarter. I have found this to be necessary in order to have a plan and an outlook and a portfolio that are reflective of both macro and micro trends and events.

uld start to build your plan at any time of the year so long
yourself a good six weeks of researching and watching the market before you start investing. Once I hit Black Friday
(the day after Thanksgiving), I begin in earnest to put together my
strategy for the coming year. In fact, I schedule an 8:00 a.m. conference call with my team at Virtus Investments (my current firm)
to go over the plan within a few days of Black Friday. That's the
perfect time to do so since not all that much happens in the financial markets between then and the end of the year. With about five
weeks before the end of the year, it is an ideal time to begin gather-
ing the research you will need to put together a coherent plan.

How do you know what to put in your investment plan? The
key is to start with the big picture by identifying macro trends
that likely will have an impact on the financial markets in the year
ahead. What will you need to monitor on a consistent basis, and
what can you set aside?

In order to put together a plan, you need to be able to answer
certain questions. I am a big believer of making sure that you see
the forest for the trees. That's why I suggest you start by answer-
ing these types of questions:

• **Where is market sentiment right now?** Is it in an uptrend
or a downtrend? Is it overly optimistic or pessimistic? If it is the
former, asset prices might be overvalued. If it is the latter, markets
might continue to be weak, or there might be signs of a reversal
and an opportunity in the very near future. If you determine that
the market has run up too quickly, you might want to be underinvested until sentiment shifts. However, if markets appear attractive
because the market is down, say, 2,000 points in the last quarter,
a turnaround might be close at hand. There is a saying that "bull
markets climb a wall of worry." That's because when people are
worried, they usually keep a lot of money on the sidelines. Once
any kind of good news hits, there is ample capital out there to fuel
a market rally.

• **How is the global economy doing?** How is China, one of the countries fueling global growth, doing? What about other key countries, such as Germany? Germany is a pivotal country to watch. If you look back to the European debt crisis in May 2010, everyone was worried about Greece, Portugal, and Spain. However, I was rather adamant that the United States would work our way through that headwind. I really wasn't concerned about it. The reason why I took such comfort is that the strongest link to the U.S. economy in the European zone is Germany, and the economic numbers out of Germany during that period suggested to me that the problem was contained to those few countries like Greece and Spain. As Germany goes, so goes Europe. An analysis of other countries will help you navigate your way through your plan. If you do not know which countries are experiencing the greatest growth, then any investment plan you attempt to write will be incomplete at best and way off the mark at worst.

• **Is fiscal policy coming out of Washington favorable or restrictive to the stock market?** Are new policies out of Washington encouraging or discouraging growth? Sometimes it is difficult to know, since there could be different types of programs all in effect at the same time—some that are good for the market and others that are bad. You need to see how the market is reacting to these programs, or if the markets are ignoring these policies altogether. Favorable programs would include lowering taxes, government stimulus packages, and regulation that encourages global trade, to name a few. An illustration of the market having a bad reaction to news from Washington was the events of the late summer of 2011. On July 25, 2011, it became clear that Congress and the president would not be able to adopt the necessary fiscal measures to reduce the long-term deficit enough to avoid the country's AAA credit rating being downgraded by S&P, one of the three major rating agencies. On that July day, the S&P 500 was trading at 1344.32. Because of the unfavorable fiscal policy emanating from Washington, and the subsequent downgrade by S&P, the market declined over the next nine trading sessions to 1101.54—roughly an 18 percent drop.

- **Is the Fed helping to increase liquidity, or are they in a tightening phase where they are restricting liquidity?** The Federal Reserve, better known as "the Fed," is the central bank of the United States. It sets the monetary policy (interest rates), regulates the banking system, and maintains the soundness of the nation's financial system. The key for investors is how the Fed manages the country's interest rates. Equities do better during easing (that is, when rates are being lowered) and usually do not perform well in the transitional phase between easing and tightening policies (*tightening* means "raising interest rates"). This is critical and relatively easy to monitor.

- **What about the value of the U.S. dollar?** The value of the dollar is a critical factor in figuring out what is happening in the overall economy. Let's say the U.S. economy is challenged and struggling for growth. The only way to stimulate growth is by cheapening currency to make goods and services globally more attractive to other nations to buy. That is why most countries try to devalue their currency: to increase total revenue for their goods and services from abroad (demand generally goes up when prices go down). Companies that do a significant amount of their business overseas (say, 40 percent or more) are likely to benefit from a weak dollar. However, if your economy is doing well—growing by, say, 4 to 5 percent—you want it reflected in the strength of your currency. In that instance, people want to own your currency. They want the capital that flows into your currency. They want that extra yield. A strong dollar and a strong GDP—really the most accurate measure of Main Street's standard of living—mean a strong economy. Absent that strength, the overall stock market benefits from a weak dollar.

- **What is happening with commodities?** I tend to look at precious metals, oil, base metals, and natural gas. Unfortunately, there is no valid index or metric that investors can watch as a benchmark for commodities. However, since 2002, investors typically use the dollar indexes as indications of where commodities should be (if the U.S. dollar is weak, commodities should be strong). It is important to note, though, that this likely will change in the future.

I also think that within the framework of my strategy, I understand seasonality and how to play seasonality. What do I mean by that? Let's look at oil. Oil historically tends to be weak during the first quarter of the year. Generally, if you look back on it, the most vulnerability in the commodities space is in the beginning of the year, and that includes gold. I also pay particularly close attention to copper. That's because copper is the metal most used in building the infrastructure of growing countries like China and Brazil. In fact, market pros call copper "Doctor Copper" because it is the asset most indicative of a strong global economy.

• **Are bonds strong or weak?** The bond market historically indicates where the equity market is going to be three months from now. The bond market is a leading indicator. The entire bond market. However, most pros look at the ten-year treasury. If you begin to see treasury yields aggressively decline, that means that there is something out there that is concerning not just retail investors, but governments, global governments, institutional investors, and so forth. That is why they are buying treasuries: to seek out the safety of the United States government debt, which in terms of credit quality is the highest in the world. We saw a dramatic shift in ten-year treasury yields back in September 2008 when they sunk to yields around 2 percent. Yields below 3 percent often indicate a weak domestic economy. This drop in bond yields was a leading indicator of the losses that were coming to the overall stock market. It was a leading indicator again when back on July 11 of 2011, the ten-year treasury closed below 3 percent. During the summer of 2011, treasuries foretold what was about to happen in the equities market, the S&P downgrade, and the tumult that we saw in the markets from the end of July through August. In fact, by August 18 of 2011, the treasury was trading below 2 percent. When treasury yields decline so aggressively, people are buying them because they are a safe haven. When that happens, the stock market usually falls: demand for stocks decreases as the demand for treasuries increases.

These are just a few of the more important macro questions investors need to answer in order to put together a comprehensive investment plan. Investors who do their due diligence and spend the majority of their time researching and planning before they actually invest likely will find that a number of macro themes overlap with one another and concurrently affect the markets as well as individual assets. For example, if market sentiment is pessimistic, there might be a lot of cash on the sidelines, poised for a rally. And if the Fed acts to ease liquidity, those two themes taken together might mean a buy sign for investors who are ready to put their cash back in the markets.

Understanding how macro themes affect the markets individually and how they work in tandem will help you learn to recognize buy signs. Once you get a handle on the macro themes affecting the capital markets, you will need to drill down into industries, individual securities, commodities, and so forth.

## Investing in the Decade of the Emerging Market

While the United States economy continues its sputtering recovery, savvy investors not only need to understand macro themes that affect the markets, they also need to look at emerging markets as opportunities for strong returns. Emerging markets are, in many respects, leading the way.

As I mentioned in the Introduction, I did not view the decade of 2000–09 as the Lost Decade, as so many pundits have called it (the S&P 500 lost about 10 percent in that period). I saw it as the Decade of the Emerging Market. Before diving further into specific investment ideas, I want to explain what I mean by this macro trend and show why this thesis is so important in constructing my investment plans. This macro view has had a major influence over my investing strategy in the past, and the next phase of this thesis will have a major impact on my future plans and investments.

Long before the end of the 2000s, I determined that the first decade of the twenty-first century was not about falling stock prices, as so many market experts concluded. Instead, I saw it as the Decade of the Emerging Market. What was the evidence for such a claim?

In retrospect, we know that in 2000, emerging market economies like Brazil, Russia, India, and China, to name a few, grew by a double-digit rate. That makes sense since these four developing countries—known as the BRICs—were building out their infrastructure. These countries are building roads, bridges, technology, office buildings, housing, etc. In order to do all of these things, these countries require energy to support production, as well as copper, the base industrial metal that goes into building the aforementioned infrastructure. That is why both oil and copper fared very well during the 2000s, even when the majority of U.S. stocks struggled. This was a classic case of the emerging world industrializing itself. Any country in its infancy is almost sure to grow by rates that dwarf those of developed countries (like the United States). Emerging countries are going to have GDPs (gross domestic product, which is the total worth of all of a country's goods and services) in excess of 10 percent. One would have to go back a very long time to come anywhere near that level of growth in the United States.* From 1947 to 2010, average quarterly GDP growth has been 3.31 percent. GDP hit an all-time high of 17.20 in March 1950. More recently, the United States had GDP

---

* As the United States was coming out of its Industrial Revolution, growth in America was strong. Between 1869 and 1879, real GDP in the United States grew at a rate of about 7 percent and grew at that rate again in the 1880s, according to noted economist Milton Friedman. These rates are below the growth rates of the emerging markets of the 2000s.

growth of 10.90 percent in the second quarter of 1983; but that was for a single quarter and not a full year.

All of this growth from the developing world does not come without a price, and that price is double-digit inflation in the BRICs. The most important piece of evidence that confirms the Decade of the Emerging Market is the price of gold. The most tangible thing the central banks in these countries could do as they build their infrastructure is to buy gold as a hedge against high inflation. That has been the action taken by many governments over the years to stave off the inflation of its currency, because high inflation is a natural by-product of expansive, aggressive growth.

As a direct result, gold became a classic buy-and-hold asset from 2000 to 2010 (with its best years from 2003 to 2010; see figure 2.1). Just because buy-and-hold has been revealed to be a flawed investment strategy in general during the last decade does not mean that there were not a few assets that could be bought and kept without experiencing significant pullbacks, and gold was one of the standouts.

Investors aren't the only ones to use gold as an inflationary hedge. Emerging countries often do the same. During the Decade of the Emerging Market, China led the pack. Around 2003, China emerged as a major economic power and a country of great interest for the United States and other developed economies around the globe. As you can see from figure 2.1, gold just went straight up for most of the decade as investors and emerging markets used gold as a hedge. There is a parallel to the United States of the 1970s when central bankers in America were aggressively buying gold to protect themselves against inflationary pressures in the economy (in the 1970s, America had interest rates of about 20 percent).

Today, emerging markets continue to protect themselves against inflationary pressures, which are a natural by-product of double-digit GDP growth. They protect themselves by diversifying their currencies and owning gold as an inflation hedge. (That gives further credibility to my assertion that the last decade was

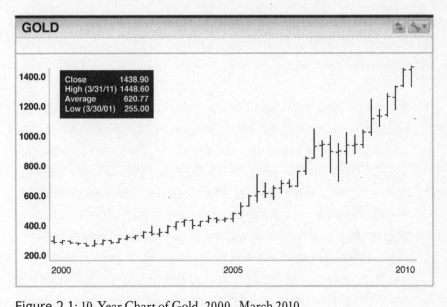

Figure 2.1: 10-Year Chart of Gold, 2000–March 2010

the Decade of the Emerging Market.) As you will see later in this chapter, my recent investment plans were built on the foundation of this important, long-term trend.

There is a second generation to the Decade of the Emerging Market, and that is the advent of the Emerging Market Consumer. Once roads, buildings, bridges, and all other key infrastructure are built, the focus will shift to the emerging market consumer. As developing nations grow, there is a natural by-product: a burgeoning middle class that wants many of the same things that the middle class citizens have in Western economies. They want the same goods and services that people in the United States enjoy, like a better diet, new appliances, better health care, credit cards, computers, iPhones—the list goes on and on. Companies that can help these developing nations satisfy the growing demand of the new middle classes will be the winners in the decade ahead. This second reality will inform and be a vital part of my future investment plans.

In July 2010, Luis Alberto Moreno, who recently was reelected president of the Inter-American Development Bank, reinforced this Emerging Market Consumer story when he was quoted in the *The Financial Times*:

> Financial analysts point to a...set of indicators that should capture the world's attention. Economic growth in Latin America and the Caribbean is forecast to average 4.5 per cent this year, twice the estimated US rate and four times faster than the Eurozone....This economic role-reversal is no accident....Over the past 20 years the region has undergone a quiet but profound transformation....Brazil is the most visible example: it has emerged as an industrial and agricultural powerhouse while lifting some 30m [million] of its citizens out of poverty, and is on track to grow more than 7 percent this year. But Brazil's progress is echoed, to varying degrees, by most of its neighbors....Latin America now has the opportunity to join Asia in leading a global economic recovery.[*]

Moreno also predicted that emerging market countries will come to the aid of developing nations and spark stronger global growth. The op-ed piece also pointed out that the growing middle classes will be at the epicenter of the lion's share of the growth coming from these countries.

## Identifying Areas of Strength in the Market

Once you get a firm handle on the global picture and macro part of the plan, then you will need to drill down to street level to complete a comprehensive plan. At the beginning of the year, you need to

---

[*]Luis Alberto Moreno, "Welcome to the Latin American Decade," *Financial Times*, July 6, 2010. Retrieved November 18, 2010, from http://digital.olivesoftware.com/Olive/ODE/FTUSEDU/LandingPage/LandingPage.aspx?href=RklULzIwMTAvMDcvMDc.&pageno=Nw.&entity=QXIwMDcwMg.&view=ZW50aXR5.

determine what kind of stocks and other investments you want to own. Will you be including commodities like gold and oil in your plan? Or will you stick strictly to equities? Do you want bonds to be part of the plan? Do you want to be in the technology space, or do other sectors look like better opportunities? Where do you see the opportunities? Where do you see potential merger or acquisition activity that could be a sign of an active sector with good upside possibilities? Where do you see dividend buybacks, which is another healthy sign of a strong company? You have to have all of this outlined ahead of time, meaning that you need to do the due diligence ahead of time. You need to have work already prepared so you can react accordingly during the course of the year.

This is where some real analysis is required. You need to search for pockets of strength within the overall stock market. The best way for individual investors to do this is to analyze the ETFs (exchange traded funds) that I have listed below (remember that an ETF is a basket of stocks that represents an index, a country, a commodity, etc., but trades like a single stock). In 2011, there are more than one thousand ETFs (up from only ninety-five in the year 2000). ETFs have assets in excess of $1 trillion (as a comparison, there are $8 trillion in U.S. mutual funds).*

In this part of the plan, we will focus only on equity ETFs by sector and not on bond or commodity ETFs (I will deal later with how to approach bonds and commodities). I am a big believer in focus and, of course, no one could analyze a thousand ETFs. The key here is to figure out which parts of the stock market you want to be in for the foreseeable future (at least until something meaningful alters the dynamics of a sector or the market as a whole, such as the Fed moving from an easing policy to a tightening policy in the first quarter of the year).

---

*Andrew Bary, "ETFs Everywhere," *Barron's*, November 15, 2010. Retrieved November 29, 2010, from http://online.barrons.com/article/SB50001424052970204425904575605030063544 648.html#articleTabs_panel_article%3D1.

While some analysis is required to analyze the ETFs as well as largest stocks within each of the ETFs below, I have narrowed the field from more than a thousand ETFs to seven. In the last few years, I concluded that the following ETFs represent the key sectors that I believe are the ones that should be analyzed and monitored by investors when doing a sector-by-sector analysis. Each of these select ETFs represents a portion of the S&P 500. The ETF for the entire S&P 500 is called Spider, (or "SPDR"), so each of the seven below are called Select SPDRs, since they represent only a select portion of those 500 stocks. I believe the following ETFs provide investors a great way to get exposure to those areas of the market that already are showing strength—or are expected to— because of one or more assumptions made from the macro analysis of the market as a whole.

- **XLK: Technology Select Sector SPDR** gives investors access to technology and telecom services. Its three biggest holdings are Apple, Microsoft, and IBM.[*]
- **XLI: Industrials Select Sector SPDR** includes large industrial firms, aerospace/defense firms, capital equipment manufacturers, and transportation companies. Its three largest holdings are General Electric, United Technologies, and UPS.
- **OIH: Oil Service Holders SPDR** gives investors exposure to U.S. oil drillers and services. There are other energy ETFs, but this is the one that gives investors the best insight into the future price of oil. Its three biggest holdings are Schlumberger, Baker Hughes, and Transocean.
- **XLY: Consumer Discretionary Select Sector SPDR** includes stocks that are linked to consumer discretionary spending and will fare well in strong economic times. Its three biggest holdings are McDonald's, the Walt Disney Company, and Amazon.

---

[*] These were the top three holdings for each ETF at the end of 2010.

- **XLB: Materials Select Sector SPDR** is a bit of a mixed bag. It provides investors with access to several sectors with a larger sector. More than half of this ETF is chemicals, then metals and mining, and paper products. Its three largest holdings are Freeport McMoran Copper and Gold, E. I. du Pont, and Dow Chemical.

- **XLP: Consumer Staples Select Sector SPDR** includes stocks that are considered less dependent on a strong economy than, say, Consumer Discretionary stocks. Its three biggest staple names are Procter & Gamble, Philip Morris International, and Walmart.

- **XLV: Health Care Select Sector SPDR** gives investors the chance to own top-quality health-care companies in the United States and Canada. Given the aging of America and the high costs associated with health-care costs for the elderly, many experts believe this to be a good long-term play. Its three biggest holdings are Johnson and Johnson, Pfizer, and Merck.

Now that I have given you the key sectors, you need to do some work in analyzing each of these so that you can determine if one or more of these are ETFs that you want to own (charting these against their 200-day moving averages, as shown in chapter 1). In addition to analyzing each ETF, I also suggest that you analyze each of the three top holdings in each of the sectors.

For example, let's look at the XLB. Year to date (end of 2010), the XLB is up 15 percent. The top holding is Freeport-McMoran (FCX), which is up 46 percent. DuPont (DD), which is the second-largest holding, is up 47.9 percent. Dow Chemical (DOW) is up 23.49 percent. Each of the top three holdings is outperforming the XLB.

I personally prefer to own the best stocks within a sector rather than buying an entire sector, but for individual investors it is probably easier to buy a sector ETF. You can make your own decisions on this: own the ETF or buy components of these (remember, I recommend owning between nine and twenty-two securities, including ETFs).

There are country-specific ETFs, as well. For example, the ETF EWH captures the top stocks on the Hong Kong market. EWC will give you exposure to the top Canadian stocks, and EWS is the symbol for the Singapore ETF. Here is where my investing philosophy differs from many experts, and this is likely to surprise you, since I am such a believer in emerging markets. I do not think that anyone should own a country-specific ETF. That is simply not the best way to get exposure to key emerging markets like Brazil, China, or Latin America, to name a few. Later in this chapter, I will explain why I feel so strongly about this investment philosophy.

## Keep Your Plan Current

You will need to reassess your investing plan either monthly or quarterly, depending upon the economic and global market trends, the industries you are monitoring most closely, the companies you are holding or thinking of buying, etc. (I do a monthly calendar of the biggest economic environment events every month and will show you what that looks like in chapter 3.)

Your plan also needs to incorporate a time element. For example, I decide at the front end that if I don't see results in, say, four months, then I may decide to exit that position and move to an area with more strength or momentum. That's where the great majority of investors make their biggest mistake. Most investors look to see if they are making money or losing money on a particular investment, but seldom know how long they have held that particular security. I have found that the majority of long-term investors hang on to their losers for years. You need to decide how long you will give each investment before cashing out, understanding that there is a definite time value to your money, which means that there is an opportunity cost to leaving your money parked in a nonperforming asset.

One more caveat: another mistake that most retail investors make is they forget that they are part of a team. (This is so critical that I devoted an entire chapter to it: chapter 4.) You should not rely on yourself to gather all of the information you need. Others can bring new intelligence and fresh perspectives that enhance your "investor quotient" (i.e., your maturity and experience as an investor). Rely only on yourself and you will diminish your potential for success. For example, one member of your team might tell you that the growth numbers coming out of China have been disappointing for two months in a row. That's a vital piece of macro intelligence that you need to know in order to put together your plan. These same members of your team also can help you analyze information and make decisions about the information as well.

### Headwinds and Tailwinds

In early 2010, when I looked to the future, I saw many headwinds that could easily be inserted into anyone's investment plan. Headwinds are things the market has to fight against; tailwinds help propel the market.

One of the key indicators is growth in the United States. I see modest GDP growth in the United States for the next two to three years. I also acknowledge that America is experiencing a structural change in unemployment. Companies have become far more productive, doing more with fewer people. So companies have little incentive to go out and hire, especially in these challenging times. In addition, there's too much uncertainty in terms of tax policy and health-care reform, complicating the employment picture even further. As a result, unemployment remains uncomfortably high at near 10 percent.

What other headwinds can limit stock market upside? Consumer spending is going to be weak for years to come. Housing will remain deeply troubled for the foreseeable future. House values aren't going to rise in any meaningful way for years to come.

I also see a lack of credit demand on the part of consumers; consumer balance sheets in need of repair (meaning that many owe more than they have); the potential for a monetary policy mistake here in the United States; the potential for a fiscal policy mistake here in the United States or in the Eurozone; and the potential for the Euro banks to have a debt crisis, to name a handful.

These are all legitimate headwinds to the markets, but you cannot focus on five to ten headwinds at once. No one can. If you did, you would never put a dime in the market.

That is why I urge investors to choose only a single headwind to worry about at any one time. In late 2010, I worried about only one thing: that the United States wouldn't have the political will to do what was necessary to sustain the recovery—that we were going to make a fiscal policy mistake, such as failing to extend the Bush-era tax cuts. In summer 2010, the market anticipated a large selling event in the third and fourth quarters on the notion that the Bush-era tax cuts would not be extended for everyone. But the numbers I saw suggested that the recovery was too nascent for the Obama administration and Congress to make that fiscal policy mistake. (As it turned out, I was correct; the tax cuts were extended.)

Having an understanding of the reaction of the equities market allowed me to translate that into a moneymaking opportunity. I was able to understand that fear and profit from it. And I was not the only one who had that fear.

On March 15, 2009, Fed Chairman Ben Bernanke appeared on the TV magazine show *60 Minutes*. It was a seminal interview because he exuded confidence in the American economy. It was, in my judgment, as important as the interview Warren Buffett gave that same month, but for different reasons. After the Bernanke interview, the markets picked up on his optimism and rallied from that point on. He finally gave the investing world what it so desperately needed: confidence. And confidence was something that we were clearly lacking until that interview. From that point on, U.S.

markets reversed course—from Armageddon to a dramatic recovery in 2009. But during that interview, when he was asked about his biggest fear, he responded that he feared that we did not have the political will to do what was necessary to sustain the recovery. That's my biggest fear as well, and it's the one fear that I take into account when I am planning and investing.

What are some of the tailwinds that can encourage you to become more fully invested? I see several promising tailwinds that can propel the stock market upward in the early part of the 2010s. The strength of corporate balance sheets is a key tailwind. (Balance sheets measure a firm's assets, liabilities, and shareholder equity. Most have been repaired since the 2008–09 liquidity crisis.) There also have been meaningful leaps in corporate productivity, as companies have been forced to do as much work with fewer people (remember that unemployment was near 10 percent for much of 2009 and 2010).

There also has been the contribution from emerging markets, as their need for natural resources has surged in recent years. That is one of the reasons we have seen such an increase in demand for resources like copper and oil.

Last, we have seen real strength in the tech sector, and the numbers tell the tale. From the end of 2008 through the end of 2010, the returns of the one hundred largest NASDAQ stocks—the ETF QQQQ represents the largest one hundred names—have roughly doubled the returns of the S&P 500. This great surge in the NASDAQ, of which 45.97 percent is technology stocks, makes sense when one analyzes the events of the past decade.

As a result of the tech meltdown in 2000–02, most NASDAQ stocks lost more than half their value, and in many cases the losses were even greater (the NASDAQ reached 5,000 in early 2000 before plummeting to about 1,200 in 2002). As a result of that crisis, it was the technology companies that were first to get their houses in order. They've been through rough times before, so during the liquidity crisis of 2008–09 they kept their inventories lean, they didn't extend credit, and they kept their labor force relatively low. It is like a neighborhood that experiences a hurricane versus a town that has not. The neighborhood that got hit by the hurricane makes sure they are ready for the next one. They know the damage that can be done, so they are first to secure the key infrastructure when the next hurricane looms. That is what happened with the tech sector, and it explains why the technology stocks weathered the liquidity crisis more effectively than the 500 S&P stocks. From November 2008 to November 2010, the S&P was up by about 40 percent while the top 100 NASDAQ stocks were up by more than 80 percent. One does not often see that degree of disparity between two major market indices, and in this case it tells us a real story that is important and timely and should be taken into account in most investment plans.

## My Investment Plans: From the Macro to the Micro

I do have one advantage over individual investors in that as a chief market strategist for a major investment company, my job description calls for me to write plans, outlooks, and white papers, and to blog about the capital markets on a consistent basis (you can find past posts and my most recent thinking at www.virtus.com). Though you likely won't be writing about investing, in order to become a more effective investor you still will need to monitor certain trends, metrics, and indicators, and answer important questions in order to devise an overall strategic approach to the market.

In this section, I share some of the things that I have put in my plans in recent years. This is for illustrative purposes, and not for you to apply to next year's plan. Global events occur too quickly for a book to give you an actual plan to follow. The point is to show you the types of things you should be focusing on in your plan.

As we were beginning to see the ending of the most recent liquidity crisis in March 2009, for example, I devised a plan I called "Embracing Pessimism." This plan was written and posted on my blog in April 2009.

*Embracing Pessimism*

In this quarterly outlook, I started with this upbeat pronouncement:

> Crisis, panic, overreaction. It doesn't matter which particular crisis we're talking about. Historically, when operating in a market environment of rising or declining prices, you'll find that people tend to panic and react the same way, every time.

I then summed up my perception of market sentiment and its ramifications for the stock market (this is condensed to feature the highlights):

> What actually occurred in the first quarter of 2009 was the embracement of the true reality and scale of the challenges we were facing—challenges not only in the market, but economically, impacting the entire financial system. The realization set in that we should expect more market losses to unfold. Clearly, the economic numbers and earnings guidance were going to look terrible. Pessimism finally reigned supreme in Q1.

I also noted the following, which I will condense down to bullet points (your plan need not be a drawn-out diatribe on the market; instead, bullet points can work just fine). Here is how I viewed things going into the second quarter of 2009 as the United States was showing signs of coming out of its great recession:

• **A time to be greedy:** I noted an important interview that took place on March 9, 2010, when Warren Buffett declared that he was still fearful of the market. I knew that it was an important moment, and time to live by the market tenet "be greedy when others are fearful, and fearful when others are greedy." There is no more important investor than Buffett. I was surprised at how fearful Buffett came off in that interview. I concluded then that it was time to step back into the market by becoming more fully invested (that is when I bought more assets, bringing my total number of holdings stocks closer to twenty-two stocks than nine).

• **The end of pessimism**: I discussed the historic opportunity presented by the liquidity crisis of 2008–09. Pessimism had bottomed and the world was underinvested. That would drive the market higher in the year ahead. In the next three to five years, the costs of housing, food, health care, and energy will clearly be higher than they are today—much higher.

• **A resilient global economy**: Emerging economies showed surprising resiliency throughout this crisis. Brazil, India, and China are beginning to restock their commodities. On the day the S&P hit a low of 665.75 in March 2009, China announced its growth target would be 8 percent for the year. The China PMI in February 2009 was the highest it had been since July 2008. (The China Manufacturing Purchasing Managers Index, reported by the Chinese Federation of Logistics and Purchasing, is an indication of whether the manufacturing economy is expanding or contracting.) In the midst of the global economic crisis, the rest of the world (not counting Eastern Europe) had remained fairly resilient and a driver of growth. The Chinese banking system was in far better shape than ours and, as such, will be another contributing factor to the ongoing recovery, in particular lifting four key sectors: health care, food, housing, and energy.

• **Demand is real**: The massive amounts of liquidity recently injected into the economy may not produce an inflationary sting for years, if at all. The concerns that I had are more about deflation. Commodity prices weren't going up out of inflation concerns; they were going up because there was an underlying concern about how producers would manage to expand future supply. Commodities were not going up because of a fear of inflation three to five years down the road—otherwise the price of gold would have topped $1,500 an ounce. This is a supply-and-demand concern more than anything else—and that is a wholly investable theme. The opportunity we see before us now may truly be historic.

## Turning Research into Strategy

In 2009, I saw energy and other natural resources as great places to invest as valuation of these commodities grew quite attractive. I also reiterated my emphasis on energy. I noted in a white paper that "the U.S. continues to import 60 percent of its oil. Until this administration develops a reasonable strategy, investment in energy—across the broad energy landscape—remains one of the top themes for investors."

I saw 2009 as something of a replay of the 1930s, when stocks had been beaten up so badly there were many opportunities for investors. This shows that you don't always have to buy high; it is rare, but sometimes the markets do still allow you to buy low and sell high, and those moment must be seized upon. I saw a "W-shaped recovery" and urged investors to get ahead of the opportunity. I felt strongly that investors needed to get off the sidelines by the second quarter of 2009 and not wait for the sharp upswing I felt would come later in 2009. I suggested that investors analyze their portfolios and buy into energy, basic materials, and commodities, as these would be the areas that would spark the impending revival.

In the second quarter of 2009, I did a strategic update and noted that by the end of June, emerging markets were up 40 percent for the year. I recommended that investors buy into that strength. I recommended China, India, Brazil, and other South American countries such as Chile, and also wrote that these markets were likely to rebound nicely for the next twelve to eighteen months, which was the right call.

If you believe, as I do, that emerging markets are the key to creating alpha in the market, then how should you invest to realize maximum gains from markets outside of the United States?

This is important, because this is where most investors get it wrong. As I mentioned, the Decade of the Emerging Market doesn't mean that you should buy a country-specific ETF such as the Brazil ETF, the China ETF, or the India ETF. It means you buy what the emerging markets need to raise their standard of living to the level that is equal to the United States and the rest of the developed world. For example, you shouldn't buy the FXI, the China ETF, when you're investing in China. Instead, you should look at companies like Mead Johnson (MJN), which makes nutritional products for infants and children. Mead Johnson gets 15 percent of its revenue from China and 9 percent from Mexico. Only 35 percent of its revenue is U.S.-centric.

The key is not to invest in the headline equity index of an emerging market but in the companies you know and understand. In many cases, that means investing in those U.S. companies that are helping countries as they emerge and develop. For example, McDonald's (MCD) and Nike (NKE) are well-known companies that are headquartered here in the States. Most investors are familiar with these companies and understand their products. But what's also great about McDonald's and Nike is that they both have international exposure of more than 60 percent, making them part of the emerging market trend.

By 2030, the developing nations are going to spend trillions of dollars to buy the goods and resources that we have in America. We have already seen evidence of great financial growth in these countries. For example, in the first ten months of 2009, $10 billion went into emerging market government debt (meaning that those emerging nations raised that level of capital by issuing debt). In addition to that, $25 billion flowed into the Indian Bombay stock exchange from other countries. Clearly this is a trend that will only grow more prominent as time goes on.

In addition, it is important to look at the price of oil over the last ten years. It had a great decade. Why? Again, it comes from the changes taking place in an emerging world that wants to move at the very least into middle-class status. They want better energy, technology, and services. Those actual goods and services—those physical assets—are the things you want to invest in, not in the country ETFs.

* * *

Now that we have 20/20 hindsight, let's take a look back at my 2009 plan and extract the key lessons for investors going forward. In March 2009, with that Warren Buffett interview, I noticed that something significant had changed. When the world's most visible investors gets fearful, I knew that something big was happening. It was recognizing that moment, recognizing its significance, which helped me to have my best year ever as an investor.

You may ask why this is relevant now. First and foremost, traders and investors have to be able to change. That's one of the biggest problems with the market right now: a financial industry that is unwilling to change. In 2000, the marketing materials generated by Wall Street revealed that few were prepared for the Decade of the Emerging Market or the decade of gold and commodities (both emerging markets and commodities outperformed the U.S. stock market dramatically between 2000 and 2010). That's why so many called that period the Lost Decade. Even professional investors weren't prepared for it. They're trying to prepare themselves right now.

One of your greatest assets as an individual investor is the ability to change and adapt when the situation calls for it. I actively seek change and do my best to stay ahead of the most meaningful changes. This entails finding new information all the time. I have a relatively simple way of dealing with new ideas. I draw a circle—two circles, in essence—of what I know and what I don't know. When I learn something new (say, a guest comes on *Fast Money* and tells me something I don't know), I write down the idea in the appropriate circle, and that becomes an actionable idea for me, something I can either act on almost immediately or investigate further.

The other important lesson of that period was that it provides a proven blueprint of how an investor should position himself when coming out of a terrible bear market. That's critical in these times, when we have volatile markets that can go up or down a thousand points during the course of just a few weeks. What if there is a geopolitical disaster? What if another war was to start in the Middle East? What if Pakistan went to war with India? What would happen to the market if another tragic terrorist plot succeeds, even if it is far from U.S. borders? Anything like this could trigger a seismic dislocation in the stock market. Even a significant slowdown in China could spark a huge sell-off. Investors have to be ready for anything, and they must have a plan that protects their downside on both sides of such an event.

# 3

# Keep an Investing Calendar

Natural disasters and political revolutions are just some of the unpredictable events that can put even the best investment plan in jeopardy. But there also are plenty of regularly scheduled events, such as meetings of the Federal Reserve's Board of Governors, that the "buy high, sell higher" investor can track and use to turn a tidy profit.

Just like your spouse and you may keep a social calendar or a calendar showing when the kids have to be at soccer practice or guitar lessons or whatever, your monthly economic calendar should become the business calendar for your investing plan.

This calendar will help you keep track of the economic events that have the power to move markets, and it can help you keep track of actual times when you should be investing, including when to get in and when to get out of investments (we'll talk more about entering and exiting the market in chapter 6). Your monthly economic calendar can help you with your due diligence by allowing you to keep track of reports and data that you need to study. And it can help you implement your investing strategy.

On just about any day of any month, economic news affects the markets and where successful traders put their money. Some of these events include monthly reports and data announcements, such as Federal Open Market Committee (FOMC) meeting decision days and Department of Energy (DOE) inventory data, and other reports that can move the markets. I keep a monthly calendar that tracks the key economic events to watch (see figure 3.1 for a sample calendar that I publish on the Virtus website; for supporting commentary see the Appendix). Think of your monthly economic calendar as an investing calendar or a business calendar.

From monthly manufacturing reports to labor reports, there are a number of key events that investors should watch because these events can really move markets.

For instance, since 2009, manufacturing has led the economic recovery in the United States and abroad, so it's important to monitor major manufacturing indicators. Key events to follow when it comes to manufacturing include the release of the ISM Manufacturing Index (Institute for Supply Management Index) and the China PMI (China's Purchasing Management Index).

The Institute for Supply Management (ISM, the largest supply management association in the world) issues a report on the first working day of every month. This report examines the overall state of business in the United States, with a particular eye toward the manufacturing sector. An influential report, the ISM index is an in-depth survey of three hundred manufacturing firms. An index value of 50 is the dividing line between a growing or contracting economy. The China PMI is a similarly influential economic indicator. The China PMI figure is released on the last calendar day of each month. As a monthly gauge of China's manufacturing sector, this report actually provides a good picture of global manufacturing health. Together, these metrics provide a comprehensive snapshot of the global economy's health, as measured by industrial output.

U.S. unemployment data, released the first calendar day of every month, provides another important indicator of the direction the market is headed, and I make it a practice to monitor the

VIRTUS
INVESTMENT PARTNERS

## Is Red the Color of February?

Joe Terranova, Chief Market Strategist, Virtus Investment Partners, offers insights into some of the key economic indicators and meaningful market events to keep a close eye on throughout February.

February 2011

| Sunday | Monday | Tuesday | Wednesday | Thursday | Friday | Saturday |
|---|---|---|---|---|---|---|
| | | 1<br>10:00 AM: ISM Manufacturing Index (January)<br>Domestic Motor Vehicle Sales (January) | 2 | 3<br>Chinese New Year Begins | 4<br>8:30 AM:<br>Private Sector Jobs and U.S. Unemployment Report (January) | 5 |
| 6 | 7 | 8 | 9<br>1:00 PM:<br>10-Yr T-Note Auction | 10<br>1:00 PM:<br>30-Yr T-Bond Auction | 11 | 12 |
| 13 | 14 | 15<br>Treasury's GSE Reform Report Due Mid-Month<br>8:30 AM:<br>Retail Sales (January) | 16<br>8:30 AM: Housing Starts (January)<br>9:15 AM: Industrial Production (January) | 17<br>8:30 AM:<br>CPI<br>(January) | 18 | 19 |
| 20 | 21 | 22 | 23<br>10:00 AM:<br>Existing Home Sales (January) | 24<br>8:30 AM:<br>Durable Goods Orders (January) | 25<br>8:30 AM: GDP (Q4p)<br>9:00 AM:<br>S&P/Case-Shiller HPI (December) | 26 |
| 27 | 28<br>Will the Fed Respond Early to Banks' Capital Plans?<br>9:00 PM:<br>China PMI (February) | | | | | |

*Times shown are Eastern Standard (EST).*

Figure 3.1: A Sample Monthly Investing Calendar

Department of Labor's private sector jobs data. The monthly Employment Situation Report (also known as the labor report) is a compilation of surveys that track the labor market. It features data that show the unemployment rate, the number of new jobs that have been created, nonfarm payroll employment, the average number of hours worked in nonfarm workweeks, and the average basic hourly rate for major industries. These data can have a dramatic impact on the markets because they measure how tight the labor market really is and because the report is viewed as an overall gauge of the general direction of the U.S. economy.

In addition to manufacturing and labor data, I also keep an eye on price indexes. In particular, I watch the Consumer Price Index (CPI) and the Producer Price Index (PPI), both of which have the power to move markets. CPI measures the price of consumer goods and services. It compares what the typical household pays for specific finished goods and services to the price during an earlier period. PPI measures the price of consumer goods and capital equipment at the producer level before they are passed along to consumers. That is, it measures prices at the wholesale level rather than at the retail level. These price data are significant among inflation indicators. By monitoring these indexes, investors can get a better sense of whether inflation is becoming an issue and whether inflation is affecting prices of food, commodities, or other goods, which could have a trickle-down effect on manufacturing, retail prices, and the overall stock market, and even on particular names that are sensitive to inflation, such as consumer discretionary stocks like Disney (DIS).

During the course of a given month, a number of reports and data are regularly released. In addition to the usual reports that are released, various events may be taking place that have the potential to move markets. For example, if Ben Bernanke, chairman of the Federal Reserve, is testifying before Congress or giving some kind of important speech, traders and investors will be hanging on his every word to see whether his comments might signal a shift in fiscal policy. Monetary policy meeting minutes, issued monthly for the Bank of England, Bank of Japan, and the FOMC, also might provide some insight into monetary policy changes that could affect the global economy.

I keep a monthly calendar so that I know which events I need to watch most closely, something I recommend for every investor that wants to raise his or her investing quotient. My economic calendar allows me to know which big economic and market events I need to focus on. It's important to look ahead to each month and flag the economic events that could affect your individual investments and your overall investing strategy.

You can use an economic calendar from sources like Yahoo! Finance or MSN's Money Central or whatever, but you really should create your own. Why do you need to create your own economic calendar? Because each month, the calendar is going to change. Though the release of monthly reports will stay the same, any number of other events could be important to your individual investing plan, and so your unique economic calendar is going to be different from month to month.

For instance, in August 2010, the whole world was worried that the economy was going to slip into a second recession, that there was going to be a double-dip recession (that is, a bad quarter after a quarter or two of growth). Investors were looking at numbers from China in 2010. China was importing fewer commodities, and the numbers were horrible. Manufacturing numbers in the United States were beginning to decline. But the market rallied in September. Why?

On August 31, 2010, the China PMI number was released, and it was better than expected, alleviating the concerns of the markets. Then, on September 1, the ISM numbers came out, and they also were better than expected, again alleviating the concerns of the markets. From that point on, the market went pretty much up for weeks, giving investors the best September in years.

If you knew what you needed to look for—if you had those

events on your calendar—you would have known right then and there that that was a moment to be in the market, that it was okay to get back into the water. Though the concerns in August were that the global economy was going to suffer through a double-dip recession, in reality the numbers weren't showing that. The first few days of your economic calendar would have highlighted the key events and data to watch for, and they would have shown that the market was in a position to rally.

As you keep up with your calendar, you'll develop a better sense of what should be on it. Monthly data releases and reports are obvious. Economic data, labor data, price data, inflation data—any report that includes a release of those data should be staples on your monthly economic calendar. You also want to note when earnings season begins. If you hold stocks, you need to know when the next earnings release is for each company and what expectations are. Your monthly economic calendar should include macro and micro events alike.

## Devise a Week-to-Week Strategy

We know now that your economic calendar should include macro events and micro events. By macro events, I mean those reports and data that provide information about major economic issues like unemployment, labor, inflation, and manufacturing, which we discussed above. Micro events include things like earnings releases. Your calendar will change from month to month, especially as you do your due diligence and become more adept at anticipating which events will affect your investment strategy.

In order to understand macro events, you first have to create a calendar that looks ahead to each month. Identify five or six important macro events. For example, as I write this in autumn 2010, unemployment is challenging the economic recovery. It's important to pay attention to unemployment numbers, so the day the

Department of Labor releases the labor report needs to be a key event on the monthly calendar.

It's also important to look at the weeks surrounding the release of key economic data. If the Employment Situation Report is on your monthly calendar, you also should be looking at the weeks before that report is issued. For example, two weeks before the labor report comes out, the Federal Reserve releases something called the Beige Book. The Beige Book is published eight times a year, and it is used in preparation for the monthly FOMC meetings. Officially called the *Summary of Commentary on Current Economic Conditions by Federal Reserve District*, the Beige Book is just that: a summary of economic conditions. It's widely viewed as an indicator of what the Fed might do during its upcoming meetings, and it becomes the macro view by which the FOMC makes policy decisions. If the labor report is one of the key events on your monthly economic calendar, events like the release of the Beige Book also should make up part of your week-to-week calendar.

But it's not just macro events that should be part of your calendar. You can use your calendar to highlight micro events such as earnings releases. Your calendar also can be used to pinpoint your investing activity not just yearly or monthly but weekly.

Micro events like earnings release dates can dramatically affect the movement of individual stocks. Once earnings release dates are announced, volatility often results, meaning the price of a stock can fluctuate dramatically during the days and weeks before the actual release date. Wall Street analysts, investing pundits, and other so-called experts often start tweaking their earnings estimates, and "whisper numbers" (i.e., unofficial analyst estimates/expectations) often start cropping up. All of this can add up to price swings that could affect your investments. It's important to mark earnings release dates on your calendar in order to position yourself to act according to your investing strategy, whether that means buying or selling—or even hanging on to—a particular investment.

Your monthly calendar can—and should—be used to mark important buying and selling events. For example, let's say that your investing strategy and your overall trading plan calls for you to buy Johnson and Johnson (JNJ). Your plan calls for you to buy Johnson and Johnson over a one-month period. So you mark that on your calendar: buy 500 shares of JNJ. When the time comes, you place the order. You're not going to worry about stock price. Instead, you're making an appointment with the market to invest in Johnson and Johnson over the course of one month. For each of four weeks in a row, you buy 25 percent of the stock until you've bought 100 percent of the shares you planned for. So, if your annual investment plan calls for you to buy 500 shares of JNJ, you buy 125 shares every week for four weeks, and you buy it when your calendar tells you to because that's what your strategy calls for. This helps you to buy in at different levels, which will help you to reduce your risk going in (buying shares over time helps you to "smooth out" the buying process, rather than staking your entire investment on one moment in time).

Your calendar helps you implement planned, systematic investing. Marking investing events like this on your calendar will help you stay on track, be objective, and take the emotion out of the investing equation. In addition, this strategy helps investors become more patient, while forcing them not to put all their eggs into one basket at once.

## Just Watch, Don't Trade

Let's talk about a couple of real situations to illustrate why it is so important that investors show patience and not put all their chips in the market at the wrong times.

A lot of folks find that event days are great trading or investing opportunities. We know that event days are those instances when important economic or market-related news is issued. For example, we mentioned that a Federal Open Market Committee decision day would be considered an event day. The FOMC holds eight regularly scheduled meetings annually; other meetings are scheduled as needed. During these events, the Fed meets to decide monetary policy—that is, they decide whether they will raise or lower interest rates or leave them unchanged.

Another event day involves oil trading. Every week, the Department of Energy issues its weekly oil inventory numbers. Typically, the DOE releases those figures at 10:30 a.m. on Wednesdays. As a result, oil trading pits often are the most populated on Wednesday mornings. The DOE used to release oil inventory data after the market closed, but the exchanges realized they could make far more money in commissions and fees if the numbers were released during the trading day. The traders loved the change because it triggered far more volatility and, in turn, trading opportunities as price action jumped into high gear, opening up the trading range and creating buy and sell opportunities.

However, at MBF, we found that the results of trading on the DOE numbers were disappointing. Initially after the release of that data, my traders at MBF had a difficult time and lost far more money than they made. As a result, I instituted risk limits so my traders couldn't be long or short more than X number of contracts. They couldn't lose more than X amount on a given trade. If a trader was down X amount of money during the course of a given day, he was done. I would get calls alerting me to trading losses and other traders reaching their daily limit within minutes of the release of that number. The problem was that our traders were stepping into the market immediately after the numbers were released. They were doing a week's worth of trading in a twenty-minute window. There was no time for thinking or plotting any sort of strategic approach. Traders were jumping in and out of opportunities without cohesive plans, risking too much—and losing too much.

It wasn't difficult to determine that I had to make certain changes in order to make sure that our traders brought more discipline to the market. It is important to note that even though the release of the DOE numbers is a short-term event, the lessons apply to longer-term investing as well. What changes did I make to help avoid those trading losses that were killing our profits?

First, I made sure that I gave traders time to think about what they were doing. I forced discipline upon our traders. Rule Number One: you can't be in the pit at 10:30. They didn't like that. They were afraid they were missing out on good trading opportunities. But the rule changed that. They couldn't go into the pit until 10:45. That gave them fifteen minutes after the data had been released and the herd was trading like mad to let the information sink in and allow the trading environment to properly smooth out. I allowed them to watch what was going on, but they could not make a trade between 10:30 a.m. and 10:45 a.m. With some traders, I pushed those times back further. The lesson here was that patience and discipline are crucial when it comes to protecting the downside.

What about FOMC decision day? In some ways, this event is like the release of the DOE oil numbers. The FOMC releases their decision at 2:15 p.m. on a Tuesday or Wednesday (eight times a year). I made sure that my investors did not make any trading decisions right after an FOMC meeting. In fact, I made sure that all of our traders blacked out that day—and the following day as well. That meant that no one could make a trading decision on the day of the announcement or the day after the decision. By blacking out those two days on the calendar, I forced my traders to see how the market reacted to the decisions and prevented any of them from getting caught up in the heat of the moment. By stepping out of the picture for a day or two and letting the information sink in—and letting the market calm down—my traders were better able to take emotion out of the investing equation.

When it comes to event days like the FOMC meetings or the DOE announcements, investors should adopt the same stance as institutional money managers by waiting a couple of days and doing their homework before acting on any information. You don't want to expose yourself during a volatility spike. An institutional money manager is not going to make a radical change to his position in the minutes following an FOMC release. In fact, he's probably not going to make a radical decision the next day, either. Institutional investors have investment oversight committees they work with, and hedge funds have similar committees. Investment titan Mario Gabelli, for example, doesn't sit around the offices of Gabelli Asset Management Company Investors, a $30 billion global investment firm, and make every investment decision on his own. He works with a team. Institutional investors generally get together within twenty-four hours of an FOMC meeting or a similar event to discuss their strategies. After information from the FOMC, DOE, Department of Labor, etc., comes out, institutional investors discuss the numbers, exchange ideas, and decide what to do in light of those numbers.

What's interesting about the unemployment report released by the Department of Labor is that it lines up perfectly with one of my favorite guidelines: "Don't make Monday decisions." As I have mentioned, I don't like to trade or invest on a Monday. In fact, Mondays should be marked on your event calendar as "No-Trade Days." That's because the market may be reacting to the wrong things and pull people into some trades that may go against them the next day. I suggest that investors watch what happens Monday, but wait until Tuesday to actually invest.

As an example, on Monday, November 15, 2010, in the early morning before the market opened, investors learned Caterpillar (CAT) would buy Bucyrus (BUCY) for $7.6 billion. Both Caterpillar and Bucyrus's stocks were in the S&P 500 at the time. As a direct result, the S&P 500 Index opened higher, at 1200, and rose to 1207.43; however, by the next day, the S&P 500 sank and traded below 1175.

There is yet another important piece of data that can hurt investors who move too quickly after its release, and that is the unemployment report issued on a Friday. Generally the institutional meeting, as I like to call it, would be held Monday after the close of the markets. The investing decision usually implemented is on Tuesday. What happens on Turnaround Tuesday generally is a reversal of the price action from Monday. I want all of that information to be digested by the market before making an investment decision. But individual investors can wait long enough to digest the information and still be ahead of the large institutions.

There is another important lesson here, and this is one that some experts would disagree with: individual investors have an advantage over institutional investors. Institutional investors trade other people's money. Because of that, they have to move carefully in light of information that comes out of event days. I don't want to be an institutional money manager. I like to trade my own book, and I prefer to invest my own family money. I think most people reading this book are in the same position—they're investing for themselves and their families. Because of that, individual investors have an edge that they often don't realize: they can be more nimble than institutional money managers. Still, investors should not make snap judgments, though they can move with or ahead of the institutions that have to wait until their investment committees make a decision.

In fact, I suggest that all investors give these macro decisions a grace period before making an investment decision. Let's look at this from another perspective: What have you got to lose by waiting until the markets settle down? What is it exactly that you're missing in that time period? If an FOMC or unemployment report is released, and you suffer losses well beyond what you normally should in your portfolio, then your portfolio was flawed in its construction to begin with. Your portfolio should be able to withstand a grace period of a few minutes, a few hours, or even a few days.

So for example, and just to reiterate these investment tenets: Regarding the FOMC data, wait until the second day after the report is released to make an investment decision (if released on Tuesday, don't invest until Thursday; if released Wednesday, don't make a decision until Friday). Mark that on your monthly event calendar. On the monthly unemployment report, wait until the following Tuesday before making an investment decision. Mark that on your calendar, too.

I have been asked whether the same rules apply to earnings releases. The answer is no. An FOMC decision is a macro event, but an earnings release is not. Earnings releases are stock-specific events—micro events—so the same guidelines do not apply. Earnings releases provide a specific set of fundamental information that investors can quickly digest and act upon. This is where you can take advantage of the institution because you're more nimble. In a sense, if you make the right decision, you're going to get ahead of the institution. As a general rule of thumb, institutions are like battleships: it's difficult to move a battleship with any speed. As an individual investor, you're going to move before the large, lumbering ship, and you're not going to get caught up in those big waves that he's going to create. So when it comes to earnings releases, grace periods do not apply.

Grace periods do apply to macro events that have a binary effect on equities and bonds and currencies and commodities. By *binary effect*, I mean an event in which everything is correlated and moving in the same direction. For example, in the moments after an FOMC decision or an unemployment announcement, the market usually has a knee-jerk reaction either up or down, often by a significant margin in either direction. The whole market goes one way or the other. That's what I mean by a binary effect.

What is the overall lesson here? Patience is an essential component of successful investing. People are compulsive by nature. It's easy to overreact to events and, as a result, to overtrade. I speak from experience because there have been many instances in my career when I traded too much. It is almost always more difficult to sit on one's hands and do nothing. Today's electronic platforms, which are a relatively new phenomenon, make investors more compulsive, whether they're on an electronic trading screen or in a trading pit, or working as a day trader. Even the doctor who sees a full day of patients but ducks out of the office every couple of hours to check his portfolio with his Morgan Stanley wealth advisor is compulsive. And I know from experience that compulsive behavior will have a negative effect on your investments and portfolio performance.

By placing restrictions on my traders, I forced them to make better, well-considered decisions. You can—and should—do the same by placing similar restrictions on your own investing. Don't invest just to invest. Choose your shots carefully. Plan your monthly event calendar and use it to implement your week-to-week strategy.

4

# Build Your
# Investing Team

The world has changed in recent years, so the majority of professional traders now buy and sell in front of computer terminals rather than in noisy, crowded trading pits. This technological shift has isolated traders, which is an unfortunate development. Why? Because isolation is the enemy of rational investing. Now more than ever, professional traders and retail investors need a team. They need to pay attention to their own mental states and be open to the wisdom of others, just as great traders, including Mark Fisher, Rob Michiels, and Baruch Glaubach, have given me insights into the psychology of markets and been my teammates over the years.

To understand the perils of investing as a solo act, you need look no further than what happened when pit trading (or "open outcry," as it is known) started disappearing back in 2007. Back then I remember feeling anxious that many of the traders who worked with me at MBF would be unable to make the transition to trading on an electronic platform and would soon be out of a job. It would be hard for them to go from a cooperative, face-to-face system to an independent, solo system.

The upside of pit trading was that there was a buddy system.

Within a large pit of roughly two hundred people—mostly men, though some women—it was very open. I had implemented a buddy system, and we all knew each other's problems. Whenever we could see that one of our buddies was in a bad position, we made sure we communicated with him. We would huddle up and have a team meeting to help him get back on track. Open outcry, with its noisy, crowded trading pits and traders communicating by yelling and using hand signals, was, in its own way, a form of team investing. But the move to electronic trading changed all that.

As I feared, hundreds of traders went home, set up their home trading offices all by themselves . . . and eventually lost everything. Some of them had to sell their homes and find a new line of work in an increasingly challenging economy. The skills required to succeed on an electronic platform were not the same as those needed to succeed in an open-outcry environment. In the new electronic world, traders had to become far more versed in macro issues (such as the rate of global growth, economic events such as Fed policy, unemployment numbers, etc.). Whether managing someone else's funds or their own accounts, traders had to be able to look at investing much differently in order to make it in the new world.

One of my closest friends and one of the best traders I have worked with, Rob Michiels, was the exception. One of the reasons I think Michiels was able to make the transition is that he had learned earlier in his career the importance of having a team and having a plan.

Michiels was something of a natural when he arrived at MBF in winter 1996. Once he started to make a lot of money, though, he had a hard time reining himself in. Michiels admitted that he took on too much risk in the marketplace, which led to large trading losses. So he took several months off before coming back to work as a partner with Mark Fisher and me at MBF. He used those months to spend some time with his new wife, to travel—basically to get off the merry-go-round, which was spinning out of control.

"My instant success was much quicker than the average person down there [on the NYMEX], but once I started to become more successful, I had more equity to trade bigger [and take riskier positions], and that's where I ran into trouble," admits Michiels. "I had situations in which I would lose a lot of money and have to learn through some painful mistakes that my talent was being quick, but not necessarily being right. I was in need of discipline and money management skills. Once I became part of a team, I became a far more complete trader. It was the combination of my ability to execute on the floor and the disciplines that were put in place that made for a winning formula. I became far more successful. The team was the missing ingredient."

When the trading world was undergoing the transformation away from open outcry, Michiels went out and hired five or six guys in the business and built his own team. He took some office space in Englewood Cliffs, New Jersey, and by 2010 he had more than thirty people working for him.

Just like Michiels, the average investor needs a team. When you're sitting at a desk by yourself, your emotions can get the better of you. It's very difficult for most of us to trade electronic platforms and not get caught up in the machine, that is, to not get caught up in the hype of the market by chasing the supposed hot stocks or hot money (those stocks that are being touted by experts and talking heads as the best stocks to own). Your portfolio is not a game of Pac-Man.

I have spent most of my career managing and mentoring other traders, so the topic of investing with a team is very dear to me. Every investor, regardless of the size of his or her portfolio, needs to understand how important it is to have some kind of a team. You need to be part of a team if you are going to be disciplined enough to buy high and sell higher. An investing team can help keep you grounded and make sure that you are not making emotional decisions—or any other kind of decision—that may hurt you and your portfolio. An investing team can help keep you on track. An investing team can prod you to make better choices. Having a team in place to help you with your investments often can spell the difference between success and failure.

As Michiels says, "It is very difficult to be alone because any moments of weakness can prove devastating. Some investors tend to marry a position or stock, and when that happens, people can lose everything." To underscore his point, he describes the typical scenario where an investor buys stock at $70 per share and then watches it drop during the course of a year to $40. Most investors don't even think of getting out at $40, because they want to get their money back. "They figure twenty years from now it will be worth $200. There's no voice of reason. No devil's advocate to say, 'You know what? It was $70, now it's $62. Maybe we're wrong. Maybe we should get out and reevaluate.'"

## Why You Need a Team

Every investor should form some sort of a small investment-type club, whether a two-person team or a five-person team. One of the reasons I did so well with the vast majority of my investments in 2009 was because I worked within this team framework.

It might sound a little odd to some people who invest on their own, but it's crucial to go out and seek others whom you trust: someone who can serve as a devil's advocate and someone with whom you can share ideas. Your team helps you implement risk management strategies, which are critical to successful investing. They act as a safety net, a small group who takes the other side of the argument when it is most critical to get another point of view. The exchange of ideas can only make people better investors. If you work in isolation, and it's just you and that screen, there's no exchange of ideas and no one to watch out for you and your interests.

You come up with the strategy, you formulate the plan for the year, and you mark key events on your investing calendar—and then you share that plan with your team. At least one of your team members should have a copy of your plan. He should be the one who says to you, "The game has changed at Qualcomm. Why are you still sitting with that stock at overweight? You should be at market weight or underweight. Perhaps you should reevaluate your position." *Overweight*, *market weight*, and *underweight* will be discussed at length in chapter 7, but suffice to say here that *overweight* is when you have a big position and *underweight* is when you have a small position. Your team members should be questioning whether your positions are right-sized in keeping with your overall portfolio and your investing goals. They should be asking whether you should be buying or selling assets in order to meet your goals.

## Pulling the "Sell" Trigger

There are many benefits to investing within a team. One of the most basic involves the ability to pull the trigger, especially when it comes to selling a stock and taking a loss. Most investors freeze up at the worst possible times. That's because by pulling the trigger and taking the loss, they are, in essence, admitting failure. That's one of the hardest things to do in any facet of life, but especially in investing.

I see a real parallel between investing alone and gambling in casinos. Of course, there is the obvious gambling element to each (although the best investors really don't gamble) in that investors take a risk every time they put money to work in the markets. But that is not the most important thing the two have in common.

What's so interesting about a casino is it provides some insight into the challenge that all investors face. Once you enter and walk the floor of a casino, one of the most difficult things to do is find the exit. If you have ever been in a large casino, you know it takes forever to get out. You can find an ATM every time you want one, but you can't find an exit (or a clock, for that matter). The entire building is constructed to keep you at the table.

Another similarity between gambling in casinos and investing without a team is that like so many gamblers, solo investors have a hard time knowing when to pick up their chips and leave the table. What if you are at a blackjack table and you are ahead by $1,000? Do you cash in? Or do you tell yourself that you're on a great winning streak and that you should keep going? What if you are down by $2,000? Do you say that's enough? Or do you tell yourself that if you keep going you can get your money back?

The answer is that most people who sit down at a gambling table have no idea under what circumstances they will quit gambling and leave the place. That's why casinos take in so much money. There's no formula, no understanding of how to get up and leave the table. The same thing happens in investing. The person who holds on to stocks for years despite price volatility is even worse off than the guy in the casino who can't find the exit. And the sad truth is that the majority of investors have some stocks in their portfolios that they should have sold ages ago.

The saddest part is that in many cases this paralyzed investor understands that something has changed, yet he can't move. Every investor has faced this dilemma, me included. But if you're working with a team, and your team knows your plan for each of the assets you hold, members of your team can say, "Hey, it's time to sell. You wanted to be out of IBM when it fell below $130, remember?" Or, "I think you have too much exposure in technology. You need to cut back there."

It is always good to have someone to challenge and question you. When you think about it, people question you all the time in other facets of your life. Your spouse may ask you about a particular purchase. Business partners may question you about new clients that may take your firm in a different direction. In just the same way, the members of your investing team can help raise issues and observations to help keep your portfolio on track. In addition, a team can help in two other important ways. A team can help you learn to forgive and forget, and a team can help to keep your personal life in order.

## Forgive and Forget

One important thing that most successful traders are able to do is to forgive and forget. Who are they forgiving? Themselves. You have to be able to forgive yourself for those terrible trades, and you have to be able to forget them as well. You should learn from your mistakes—and then put them behind you. It's important to understand that even if you make a boneheaded move (or several), as long as you still have most of your capital, you can make the money back. The market will be open tomorrow, so it doesn't do any good to beat yourself up for days or weeks on end.

Let me tell you a story about one of my traders that underscores the point. Baruch Glaubach was one of the top five crude oil pit traders that I ever seen. Baruch was diminutive in size but not in stature. He was well respected. He started in the business in the 1980s and had earned the respect and admiration of the entire trading floor. One day during the volatile times of Hurricane Katrina, the oil market was moving in an extremely volatile and illogical way. The price action wasn't making much sense. An unknown variable in the market seemed to be pushing prices in an erratic fashion. The trading pits were going crazy. They were noisy and busy, and traders were buying and selling like there was no tomorrow. Amidst all this craziness, I found Baruch at the bottom of the pit leaning on a railing, just kind of taking a break. He was a very active trader, not the type of trader who would walk away from a busy market and the trading opportunities that go along with that. So I went over to him and asked what was going on with him. He responded by telling me that he really did not understand the fundamentals relative to the concurrent price action in the pits. It wasn't that he thought the pricing was wrong; it was just that he didn't understand it. I looked at him in a quizzical manner, and when he noticed my puzzlement, he shot back and asked, "Is the market closed tomorrow?"

I looked back at him, kind of curiously. I said, "What do you mean 'Is it closed tomorrow'?"

Baruch asked again, "Is the market closed tomorrow?"

I told him it wasn't.

"So what do I have to worry about?" he asked.

Baruch understood that even though he was having a rough day, it wasn't the end of the world. He knew he had to forgive himself for any mistakes he might have made today because the market would be open tomorrow. The same goes for professional traders and individual investors. The market will be open tomorrow, next month, next quarter. There always will be new opportunities. As long as you're upright, as long as you're not six feet under, then you've got a chance to be successful. You always have the chance to mend mistakes, but you have to be able to forgive yourself, forget about it, and move past any bad trades. Having someone on your team who can talk you through rough patches can help you move beyond any bad trading decisions and get you back on track.

The Baruch Glaubach story provides a great lesson for investors. When an investor does not have an understanding or the confidence of something that is happening in the market, it is fine just to sit back and not participate. In fact, it is the right thing to do. When you think about it, this lesson works on any size scale, whether it is an individual investor or a large corporation.

Take AIG, the insurance giant, as an example. AIG Financial was a small part of AIG the insurance conglomerate. When the toxic mortgage assets were developed and traded, I questioned whether they truly understood what they were getting themselves into. Did they really understand those bad assets? Or did top managers at AIG say something like *We are a huge player, a big financial player, so we have to be in it*? If AIG would have acknowledged that they didn't understand what it was they were trading, they clearly would be in a much better place today. And it isn't only AIG. I question whether the top managers of some of the biggest financial firms truly understood exactly what they were trading when those toxic mortgage products were being sold. Again, the lesson is, if you don't understand it, walk away and live for another day.

*Everything Needs to Be in Order*

In addition to forgiving and forgetting, successful investors need to have their personal lives in order, and this is another area where having a team in place can be really helpful. In order to be successful at investing, your private life must be in order. If your personal life is a mess, it can be too easy to become mired in emotions and trade without discipline.

At MBF, we knew that it was very important for us to have an open dialogue with our traders to understand when they were experiencing a personal trauma that might affect their decision making. This was especially true after the terrorist attacks of September 11, 2001.

In the wake of 9/11, there was a lot of volatility, a lot of dislocation in the markets. On Monday, September 17, the first day of trading after the attacks, there was a ceremony with then Senator Hillary Clinton, Mayor Rudy Giuliani, and Governor George Pataki on the floor of the NYMEX, which was known as "the Cove." Located right along the Hudson River, you actually had to walk through the courtyard of the World Trade Center to get there. I remember the opening bell ringing, and for a couple of seconds, it was a little bit busy. Then it just fell eerily silent. I thought, *What the hell? Why is it so quiet?*

The pits also were relatively empty. Guys were outside. They didn't want to trade. They just went for a walk. You would think it would be really busy in light of all the volatility, but most of the traders had suffered so much personal trauma that they simply couldn't trade. At that moment, there was too much emotion in their lives to make successful investing a possibility.

Of course, this level of trauma is unusual for most of us. But any amount of personal trauma can affect your trading. Your team can help you recognize when your personal life is getting in the way of successful trading, and they can help you overcome issues you may be facing. I learned this lesson for myself in 2009, and it's one of the reasons I always have a team in place to help me invest.

Two thousand nine started out as an unbelievable year for me. My best yet. But that summer, things started to fall apart. I had lost both of my parents—my mom in the early 1990s and my dad in the late 1990s—when I was much younger, and my uncle became a surrogate father to me. He and I were very close. On the evening of Friday, July 24, I called my uncle to tell him that Rick Santelli was going to be on *Fast Money*. My uncle was a huge fan of Rick, who is an on-air editor with CNBC Business News. The call began with my uncle telling me he wasn't feeling well, so we began to discuss what might be wrong with him. Suddenly I had reached Penn Station to catch the train home, so I ended the call. I never had the chance to tell him about Rick Santelli. That night, after his regular Texas Hold 'Em Friday Night Game, my uncle suffered a brain aneurysm while driving home in his brand-new electric-blue Lexus sedan.

At about eleven o'clock that night, he crashed into a fence. He was airlifted from Downingtown, Pennsylvania, to the Hospital of the University of Pennsylvania, about thirty-five miles away. About two hours later, I got a call from my cousin Susan, his daughter. She explained what happened and asked me to come get her in her apartment in New York so that we could drive down to Pennsylvania to be with him. So I got into my Range Rover and rushed through Manhattan to pick up Susan. We sped down to Philadelphia, and I can tell you that while on the Jersey Turnpike, we didn't waste much time driving less than 100 mph.

I will always remember the doctor coming out after nine hours of surgery. I wanted to thank him for saving my uncle's life. But the doctor said, "Six months from now, you won't be thanking me. Six months from now, he won't have quality of life." My uncle was bedridden. He suffered brain damage. He wouldn't be able to communicate, he wouldn't be able to recognize anyone, and he wouldn't be able to walk.

I felt like an orphan. The loss of my uncle hit me hard, and the emotions it stirred up began to poison my investing performance. Even though I was surrounded by my wife and children, I felt lost.

I talk a lot about keeping emotions in check. But, internally, I was very angry about what had happened to my uncle. My fragile emotional state was starting to tear my success into shreds. I tried to wade my way through, but it was no good. I kept taking on positions that were too large, as though I constantly wanted to pick a fight with the market. I lost my discipline. I had an attitude of *What's the difference? What do I care if I lose $25,000 or $50,000 or $100,000? What's that in comparison to the value of life?*

As a result, the next few weeks were a disaster.

By August, I was trading awfully. Recklessly. But after realizing that my personal life was affecting my trading, I just shut myself down. I liquidated most of my positions. I put myself in the penalty box for the remainder of the month of September. I didn't get out of all my positions, but I recognized that I needed a timeout. I cut all my positions down to the bare bones. I didn't make any big decisions, and I got some perspective. I reached out to people in the market whom I respect, and they helped me take a step back to soften the blow, to recover from and to process the event. They helped me protect my downside by investing less in the wake of my uncle's tragedy.

My team helped me work through the events in my personal life that were making my trading a mess. They saved me from myself. They told me no when I was making bad decisions. More so than at any other time during my career, they said, "That doesn't make sense." They told me, "That's not what you do when you make money."

At a time when just about everything I did was wrong, my team and I agreed to shut it down. I refrained from trading for nearly a month, and once that period was over, I came back knowing I had a team in place that would be able to help see me through everything I did from that point on.

*Retail Investors Need Teams More Than the Pros Do*

One could make a compelling argument as to why the individual investor needs a team more than the trading professional does. If trading or investing is someone's sole source of income, the one way that someone puts food on the table, that person has to have a skill and knowledge level that the so-called retail investor typically lacks.

The typical individual investor has another full-time job, whether a doctor or an electrician or whatever. Let's say he comes home after putting in a full eight-hour day, only to discover that the Dow has fallen 250 points. Now what does he do? The market is closed, and the next day he has to go out again and work at his day job—away from the market. To do it all on his own—to work forty or more hours a week and maybe raise a family and then try to manage a portfolio of investments all on his own—is really a terrible idea. Without the help of others, I would expect someone in that position to rack up some big losses. It's not like he has to trade every day or even every week; it's more a question of not being able to devote enough attention to the stock market and the events that are affecting it.

When you have a team of people together, investing becomes an activity you can handle—successfully. It's an activity where you search for a good idea, where you sit and discuss ideas with the one person or the two or three people that you do it with, and you say, "Okay. Let's talk about consumer discretionary. Tell me about what's going on in the retail space."

Eventually you're going to get one good idea—that one good idea that really fits in with your investing strategy—and your team can help you get there. In essence, what you're trying to do is emulate what goes on in the conference room of any good portfolio manager who sits with his team. He sits with his team, and that team is looking for one good idea.

I remember doing just that with Mark Fisher and his team in

the offices at MBF—sitting together and talking through ideas. In September 2007, a couple months after two Bear Stearns hedge funds collapsed—which actually signaled the beginning of the credit crisis that would hit in full force in 2008—we were discussing the crisis and the role of American Express, MasterCard, Visa, and Discover.

We knew that in the midst of the credit crisis, the banks were holding what would be viewed as nonperforming loans. Let me explain: When you think of credit, you think of credit cards. A lot of the nonperforming assets to come out of the credit crisis would be from credit cards—high balances that people would default on. When the credit crisis hit, everyone asked, "Wow. What happens now with Visa and MasterCard?" Their stocks had been dragged down along with the rest of the financial services sector. But what most people didn't realize is that Visa and MasterCard don't actually have credit exposure. They're just the processors. It doesn't actually matter to Visa or MasterCard if the cardholders default. It's the banks that hold the cards that are the ones who are exposed. The reality is that in times of strife, people have less readily available cash, so they actually use their credit cards more. We knew that in the midst of the crisis, Visa and MasterCard would actually do better on a relative basis.

At least ten of us were in the room just going back and forth about this. Eventually, Mark said, "I like that idea." It was one idea: to focus more on Visa and MasterCard. Mark made a decision: "I like that idea." In a way, it didn't even matter what the actual decision was. The lesson is that a good idea came out of a good conversation with a good investing team. Good ideas come out of thirty minutes of conversation.

## Your Team Is Your Investment Oversight Committee

Institutional investors have investment oversight committees that help them come to well-founded investing decisions. These IOCs review economic events, financial reports, and all types of information to determine how particular investments will affect their overall investing plans. They meet regularly to discuss tactics and strategies. They review the performances of their portfolio managers. IOCs provide institutional investors with the kind of insight that most individual investors rarely can avail themselves of.

In reality, though, there is no reason that individual investors can't form their own IOCs, and that's really what I mean when I talk about creating an investment team. You may not need to have a boardroom full of advisors, but you can have two or three or five people whose opinions you respect helping you stay disciplined, helping you forgive yourself and move beyond bad investing choices, and helping you ensure that your personal life isn't overwhelming your investment decisions.

Your personal IOC—your investing team—can help you look at what's going on in the economy and the markets. They can help you examine the performance of your individual investments. And they can help you evaluate whether your strategy is on track.

### My Team Keeps Me on Track

Just as IOCs aren't just for large institutional investors, investing teams aren't just for novices or for those with smaller portfolios. Everyone who is investing should have a team to help keep them on track. As part of executing my own game plan, I often refer back to the Virtus Investment Partners website (www.virtus.com), where I can review the ten to twelve blogs I post each month as well as my quarterly white papers. I want to be sure that I am adhering to the plan that I have written and am not going off on a tangent. I also make sure that at least one other member of my team has access to my investment plan.

I surround myself with a large investment team. A team member can be anyone with whom you exchange ideas, even on an informal basis. So my team consists of several different people who play different roles.

My financial advisor, Mike, is someone I have known for more than twenty years. We grew up together. Mike is active in the markets. He understands them. I often talk to him to exchange ideas about positions and the market in general. I also trust him to challenge my ideas and push back on those occasions when I deviate from my stated investing plan.

I also talk regularly with the lead portfolio managers at Virtus Investment Partners. In February 2011, Virtus Investment Partners' Dave Albrycht was recognized by *Barron's* as having the best taxable bond fund family in the "Best Fund Families in 2010" report. It's important to have a bond guru on your team, because fixed income has a huge impact on the capital markets. In fact, fixed income is a much bigger market than the equity market. In 2008, what really underscored the credit crisis was that the fixed-income market froze. No one was willing to issue any credit. Having someone on my team like Dave, who understands how fluid and important the bond market is, is a huge advantage. Knowing that, I have a regularly scheduled weekly call with Dave to review the credit markets and to exchange overall capital markets ideas.

I also talk to Peter Newell about the emerging markets and to Carlton Neel about natural resources, commodities, and large-cap stocks. I talk to all of these experts on a consistent basis, which is one of the keys to maintaining a successful investment team.

To show you how much confidence I have in members of my team, let me relate a story. I remember consulting Carlton on March 6, 2009, asking his opinion just before I was about to pull the trigger on a number of buys (that was around the time I wrote the "Embracing Pessimism" strategy discussed in chapter 2). Carlton has been in the financial business for a long time, as long as I have. So when we talk, it's a conversation of equals, and I really respect his opinion. Carlton is someone I know I can turn to when I need to make an important decision. On that day in March, I was looking for him to tell me why I *shouldn't* pull the trigger. The conversation I had with him was the final confirmation I needed to get back in the market in a big way.

In addition to Dave, Peter, Carlton, and others at Virtus, I also am surrounded by a great group of people at *Fast Money*, and I consider them to be part of my investment team as well. This includes host Melissa Lee, who often has a great sense of what is happening in the market (even though as host of the show she cannot buy or sell securities). If a particular sector seems to be in the spotlight for some reason, Melissa has a keen ability to discern the real news from the noise.

For example, toward the end of 2010, the Federal Reserve Board proposed rules that could have cut debit-card interchange fees by 90 percent. Shares of MasterCard and Visa declined precipitously. However, I was suspicious of the decline and thought the "selling event" might provide an opportunity. I was confident that owning best-in-breed financials like MasterCard and Visa was the right move. I remember in the days that followed, every guest on *Fast Money* seemed to be down on MasterCard and Visa, expecting their business models and earnings growth to be seriously impacted by the proposed rules. I could see in Melissa's face that she just wasn't buying into it. During the break, I leaned over and asked her, "Right here: buy or sell MasterCard and Visa?" She replied "Buy 'em," arguing that they had seen the worst of it and were poised for a comeback: "No way after all the financials have been through the past two years this takes them down," she said, which is exactly what I thought. Over the next six months shares of MasterCard and Visa both surged over 20 percent higher.

I also talk constantly with *Fast Money* co–show member Pete Najarian about options, and I have learned a great deal from him. In fact, I talk to him so frequently that I worry about taking up too much of his time. But he always seems to have time for me. Pete was particularly helpful during my uncle's crisis. During that time, I asked him about some trades I had on. I could see for the moment his focus wasn't on the actual holdings but something else. He looked at me, shook his head, and firmly chided me: "You've got too much risk on, brother." Pete could be honest with me and state the obvious, forcing me to take a long look in the mirror and helping me to recognize that I was taking on more risk than I could handle emotionally at a key point in time. It was liquidation time, and thanks to Pete I recognized it.

I also speak regularly with Tim Seymour, a hedge fund manager who specializes in emerging markets; he is also a *Fast Money* regular. Before I joined *Fast Money*, I believed in the emerging markets but wasn't sure how to trade or position for them. Tim always comes to the show armed with a barrage of key statistics, facts, and figures. Not generalities. That is so important; most business television guests like to hedge their views. They present a "thesis" that leaves the viewer scratching his head in search of a course of action. Tim talks specifics. He can present macro views along with micro actions that have helped me gain confidence in pursuing a specific course of action.

Karen Finerman has taught me about value investing and speculative risk. But most important, I find Karen's mechanical, unemotional approach to be exactly what all traders and investors should aim for. Here is a woman who could have one of the biggest egos on the Street, but she never allows it to enter the equation. That's a formula for success. The hedge fund industry has something of a black eye these days for a variety of reasons. Huge egos litter the hedge fund industry. But as a hedge fund manager, Karen is the complete opposite of that. She is incredibly focused on risk. Her knowledge of valuation fundamentals and, most important, her understanding of the critical role of management in evaluating companies are indispensable. She understands that the market can remain illogical far longer than most investors can remain solvent. Above all else, she respects the market, which brings me to the original cast member and leader of our Fast Money Five, Guy Adami.

*Fast Money* is Guy's house, and it should be. He is the lone original panelist. He is usually the first in the green room (that is a sort of locker room that we go to before the show), and the last to leave. You want commitment and preparation, and that describes Guy perfectly. Guy knows how to identify meaningful changes in the market. For example, Guy may see price action making a big move—a move that might have most investors selling in a rush. But Guy looks at the whole story, questioning whether the market is really saying something else. He has phenomenal discipline and won't take a position if he doesn't believe the whole story. Guy also respects the market. That is something that all investors must demand of themselves before putting their hard-earned money to work in the market.

I get the benefit of all of these experts' opinions, both on and off the air. We also have three conference calls each day (at 9:00 a.m., 1:30 p.m., and 4:30 p.m.) with CNBC's John Melloy, executive producer of *Fast Money*, to prepare for each night's show. John talks about what matters most to Main Street, to individual investors. He knows what they want to get out of the show, what they want us to discuss, and what they want to understand. He pushes us not only to talk about, for example, what Apple is doing on any given day but to know everything there is to know about the Apple story, about whether the story has changed for Apple's fundamentals. He motivates me to be more than prepared so I understand what is driving a particular stock. He, too, is a member of my team.

I also talk to other close friends, as well as my wife, who understands better than anyone when I take home a bad mood after a bad trading day. She helps me to keep things in proper perspective.

I also remember having a dialogue on Twitter with author and expert Anthony Scaramucci, who is a frequent guest on *Fast Money*. I was at 30 Rockefeller Center in New York City getting ready to go on the *Fast Money Halftime Report*, and we were exchanging ideas while he was in Baghdad. The conversation about the markets was nearly instantaneous, even though we were a world away from each other.

Finally, you must have someone that fills the mentor/father/ big brother role on your team. For me, obviously, Mark Fisher is an integral part of that, and he has been for the better part of twenty years in all aspects of my life. More recently, CNBC's Gary Kaminsky, whom I genuinely view as a professional big brother, has helped me quite a bit. Whoever it is that fills this role for you, it must be someone that you have tremendous respect for. Someone you want to emulate. If my trading process could emulate Mark's or Gary's, I would know that I have attained success. It is important to have someone on your team whom you look up to, someone you strive to emulate.

## Key Players on Your Team

Obviously, with my connections with CNBC and Virtus and so forth, I have access to some really smart people and am able to tap into some serious market wisdom. But that really doesn't matter— smart people are all around you, and you, too, can pull together a winning team. Your potential team members should include people already in your own circle, whether the guys you play poker with, your circle of real housewives of Main Street USA, your college roommates, or a community investing club or group.

You also could engage in a healthy dialogue with people you don't know personally, such as other investors you meet through social networking sites like Facebook or Twitter. (I am a big believer of connecting and sharing financial insights with people on social media sites.) These conversations can be an excellent barometer about real market sentiment and also can shed some light on what investors may be looking for in the market. My experience with Twitter and Facebook is that there tends to be a high-quality exchange of content and ideas, so those are the two chief go-to social sites I would recommend to retail investors. All of these interactions—whether real or virtual—can help you gauge the sentiment of the market and the investing public, as well as challenge your own strategy and thinking.

Your team also should involve at least one financial professional. The professional on your team could include a stockbroker, an asset manager, a private banker, a financial advisor, a financial planner, an accountant, and so on. For most investors, choosing a professional is a lot more complicated than choosing the amateurs—like your poker buddies or Facebook friends—who will be on your team.

What's the difference between, say, a stockbroker and a financial advisor? That's where things can get a little tricky, actually. Often, the lines are blurred.

## Choosing the Right Professionals for Your Team

Stockbrokers sell investment products, typically as a third party on behalf of a company or fund that issues stocks. Brokers make trades. Financial advisors and registered investment advisors are regulated by the Investment Advisers Act of 1940. They advise clients as to the value and suitability of investments and often issue analyses of various investments. Financial advisors are required to act in the best interests of their clients, and although stockbrokers should do so, too, they are not required to by law.

Financial planners are another animal. Whereas financial advisors are there to help you analyze specific investments, a financial planner can help you craft an investing road map. A planner might work with you to craft a strategy to reach your retirement goals, to save for your children's education, or to address tax issues.

But here's where it can get really tricky. Some financial planners also are financial advisors. Some stockbrokers bundle their services with financial-advisor-type services. The keys are to know what your planner calls himself and to ensure that he is a fiduciary (which is a fancy way of saying that he is committed to putting your financial interests first). As with selecting the individual investments that will help you meet your goals, it pays to do your homework in order to determine which type of broker, planner, or advisor is right for you.

When selecting a professional, consider some of these issues:

- **Is the professional registered or certified?** For instance, is she a certified financial planner (CFP), a registered investment advisor (RIA), or a chartered financial consultant (ChFC)? Is your stockbroker licensed? When choosing a financial professional, be sure to select someone who is educated and qualified.
- **Is the professional committed to helping you reach your financial goals?** Some professionals are there simply to sell securities to you. Make sure you get what you pay for, and if it is advice you're after—and you should be, as that's one of the roles of your team members—make sure the professional you choose is not only qualified to offer that advice but also has your best interests at heart.
- **Is the professional charging a reasonable fee?** Fees vary across the spectrum of financial professionals. Most advisors will charge a fee based on a percentage of your portfolio's value. These fees can vary anywhere from about 0.5 percent to 2.0 percent. Some might charge a commission instead of or in addition to standard fees. Some might charge an hourly rate or a flat rate. Be sure to ask the professional what she charges and how fees will be assessed.

Investors have a lot of choices when it comes to professionals who could be part of their investing teams. Chances are, though, that you may well find it helpful to enlist the assistance of a financial advisor and to make that person part of your team. In fact, I'd even go so far as to say that you should consider abandoning online trading in favor of working with a financial advisor. Sure, it may cost more (maybe $25 a trade instead of $8). But what you get for that extra money is a valuable member on your individual IOC: someone you can discuss investing ideas with, someone who knows your investing goals, and someone who understands your investing plan—not to mention someone who is committed to putting your financial interests ahead of his own.

Your investment advisor can help you actually move your money in and out of investments according to your plan. Investment advisors can help with planning, implementing, and monitoring your investments. You should utilize those services. You should develop a relationship with an objective advisor who can guide you when it comes to actually making investments.

As mentioned, choosing a financial advisor is something you should do with care. Obviously, the person has to be someone you trust, someone you get along with. You want to make sure you're aligned with a credible institution. In addition, you want to make sure that your advisor is an active investor himself. He should be able to share with you the experiences of profiting and losing. Your investment advisor has to be more than just an order taker.

Ask potential investment advisors some key questions: How do they transact? What is their system for actually inputting orders? Do they invest themselves? Are they invested in the holdings they are recommending? An investment advisor should have a relatively simple, easy system in place for conducting transactions. It should not be cumbersome or loaded with fees. An advisor should be an active investor who is invested in at least some of the same holdings he is recommending to you. If not, he should be able to explain why.

Finally, make sure that whomever you choose as an investment advisor fully understands that the minute you fail to adhere to your own plan and your advisor doesn't say, "Wait! That's not the plan we have in place!" that individual is no longer your advisor. Your advisor has to be a team player. He is there to keep you on track, to help you stick to your plan. If he is not going to do that—for whatever reason—you need to find someone else to fill his spot on your team.

### Working with Your Team

Once you have your team in place and you know you can look to your team members for help with discipline, forgiveness, and emotionless trading, you need to determine exactly how you're going to work together and what you and your team will do together. In the end, your investment decisions are your own—you can't blame anyone else for trades that go bad, and you can't let anyone else take the credit when investments go well—but you and your team should be able to rely on each other. Working with your team includes discussing ideas, analyzing trades, and challenging each other.

When it comes to investing, all your ideas can't be your own. With all the investing information, news, and noise that are floating around out there, it would be impossible to filter through it all to come up with all your own investing ideas. Your team plays a crucial role here by helping you sift through all that information. You can bounce ideas off your team members to see which investments might best fit your plan. You and your team members should read market news and investing literature and discuss the ideas that come from those and various other media.

Doing your own due diligence is a crucial part of successful investing. Your team members can help you with this by discussing economic events and how those events might affect the overall market as well as your individual investments. It's up to you to do your own legwork, but your team can help you make sense of the information you gather.

Once you and your team have discussed ideas, they also can help you analyze individual investments and the trades you make. Your team can help ensure that you've adhered to your overall plan as well as to your week-to-week strategy. If, for example, your plan calls for you to buy 500 shares of Johnson and Johnson over the course of four weeks, as we discussed in chapter 3, your team members can help ensure that you stick to the plan. They also can help you analyze down the road whether that investment is working for you or whether, as we discussed earlier in this chapter, it's time to pull the trigger and unload some or all of the shares.

In addition to analyzing your trades, you and your individual IOC should challenge each other. Although you do want team members who are of the same financial fiber, you don't want a team full of yes-men who blindly agree with all of your opinions and each of your ideas. You want team members who will tell you where you're going wrong, when you're making mistakes, and when you need to step back.

One of the worst things that can happen in any business is that you're not challenged. Success comes from being challenged by others. I don't need you to tell me where I'm right. I came up with a plan, I came up with an idea, I have conviction behind what I think potentially is right and accurate. I want to know where you think I'm wrong. Your investing team should be able—and willing—to tell you where and when you're wrong.

Investing team members should be able to tell you where you can make improvements in order to achieve the goals you outlined in your investing plan. Although they shouldn't be contrarian just for the sake of being contrarian, they should be able to question your investments and your overall plan. But there needs to be balance, and your team should provide constructive criticism to help you achieve your investing goals.

You and your team also should make it a point to discuss major events that move the market. Whether it's an earthquake in Japan or the Fed implements a new policy, you and your team should address that event within the following few days—though that doesn't necessarily mean you should buy or sell right then. You should discuss the effects that those events might have on your portfolio. You should discuss how to approach the market in light of those events.

In addition to discussing market-moving events when they occur, you and your team should plan to meet at least quarterly. Some kind of dinner or lunch or other get-together is worth having, and during that get-together the main topic of conversation should be your investing strategy and how you are doing in terms of reaching your overall investment goals.

Teamwork is about exchanging ideas. It's about offering constructive criticism. But most important, teamwork is about allowing others to point out potentially problematic conditions with a particular investment strategy that you've devised—and it's about being humble enough to listen to what your team members have to say. If your ego is so big that you're unwilling to listen to the input of your team members, then your individual IOC will be of no value. You will then, in essence, be trading in isolation, which is a recipe for disaster.

In a day and age when most Americans spend eight hours or more every day glued to their computer screens, isolation can become a big problem, and this is especially true for investors. But investing in isolation is almost always a bad idea, as it makes it easier for you to get caught up in chasing trends and hot stocks. Having a team in place can help mitigate bad habits that go along with investing alone—bad habits like trading without discipline and trading with too much emotion.

Your investing team should have a copy of your investing plan, your monthly calendar, and your week-to-week strategy. They should be prepared to challenge you—and you should be prepared to accept their challenges and learn from them. In the end, though, your investing decisions are your own responsibility. But there are things you can do to help you invest like a professional, and we'll look at some of those in the chapters to come.

# EXECUTE LIKE A PROFESSIONAL

5

# Understand Timing, Herds, and Diversification

In part I, we looked at what it takes to think like a professional trader. We explained what it means to buy high and sell higher, and why the concept of buy-and-hold investing is no longer a viable investing strategy in today's economic climate. We also discussed the importance of preparing an investing strategy—before you begin trading. We looked at the importance of creating an investing calendar and devising a week-to-week strategy. Finally, we talked about teams and why it is so important—crucial, really—to have an individual investing oversight committee to help keep you on track. Together, incorporating these approaches will help position you to execute your strategy and trade like a professional.

What does it take to trade like a professional? Training and experience for starters. Instinct, too, can help. Training and experience allow you to develop intuition, and from that comes instinct, which can help guide your investing decisions. Training, experience, and instinct come with practice. I've learned a lot over the years—from those moments when trades went right as well as from when they went wrong (mistakes are great teaching events).

Unfortunately, not every investor has the time or opportunity to spend years honing his skills on a trading floor. But adopting the good habits of highly successful pros can help anyone trade smarter and get better returns. These best practices will help you to grow beyond your current skill level. So in this chapter, we'll look at some guidelines, rules, and, yes, best practices that can help investors carry out their investing strategies. These include making the most of timing, avoiding herds and hysteria, and being diversified.

## Make the Most of Timing

Professional traders know that successful investing has a lot to do with timing. Your annual investing plan, your monthly calendar, and your week-to-week strategy—all of this relates to timing. Those are macro issues, and we talked about those in chapter 3. But timing is more than that. It also has to do with when you actually invest, when you put new money to work in the market. These are micro issues. This kind of timing means keeping an eye on quarterly trends and making sure you're keeping ahead of the game.

When it comes to timing, you also have to create a ticking clock for each investment. How much time will you give a certain stock to hit a certain price? Part of that decision process involves understanding the value of "dead money" and how dead money can be toxic to your portfolio. All of these things add up to make timing a key facet of investing that professional traders keep a close eye on—and you should, too.

### Don't Trade on Mondays (Trade on Thursdays Instead)

We've talked a bit about why investors should not trade on Mondays. Whether traders love or hate their personal lives, the pros that move markets often come into the office on Mondays in a bad mood. It may be because they can't stand to be away from home, or it may be that forty-eight hours at home has them ready to explode.

Whatever the reason, there is always a flood of emotion coursing through the market on Mondays. Markets that are trading on emotions are not where you want to be. I make it a point to never trade on Mondays. I can't tell you how full the penalty box used to be at MBF on Mondays. If I looked at each day of the week, Monday was almost always the day that traders were reaching their loss limits for the day and just trading poorly.

So when should you trade? If Mondays are no good, which days are better for investors? I generally like to execute trades on Wednesdays and Thursdays. By Wednesday or Thursday, the markets have settled down from the emotions of the weekend, and you're in front of whatever potential rebalancing could occur on Friday. A lot of hedge funds use institutional plot models that reallocate on a weekly basis, so they are rebalancing and repositioning weekly, and Fridays are when they execute that rebalance.

On Fridays you're through the cycle of what needs to be known about that week in terms of information flow, and you've not chased any of the "hot money" so that you stayed clear of the wrong stocks (we'll talk more about hot money later in the chapter). In my experience, Thursday has been my best trading day. Of course, that's not a statistical truism. It's simply been my experience, and that experience has proved itself time and time again for me. It also is something that I noticed working with the traders at MBF.

By Thursday, I've generally found, my traders got into a groove, they had a good understanding of the information that had unfolded during the course of the week, and they had a solid estimation of how the market would potentially position itself by Friday. In addition to that, they were in a good place psychologically, one in which they knew there was only one more day left to the trading week. They knew the weekend was almost there, which put them in a good frame of mind, a relaxed state of mind. By Thursday, much of the emotion has been stripped away, making for better investing and smarter trading.

Fridays also can be good trading days, but a lot of professional traders take Friday afternoons off. The main reason for this is to avoid making mistakes on a Friday afternoon that you have to carry with you until trading resumes on Monday. A bad Friday sets a bad tone for the weekend. Negative thoughts can fester over the weekend and lead to a second round of overly emotional trades on Monday. If you decide to trade on Fridays—particularly on Friday afternoons—avoid making decisions that will plague your weekends and force you into unwanted positions that you need to correct the following week.

I've been asked about what investors should do if a stock that they're holding or following has a scheduled announcement on one of your "do not trade" days like Mondays, Tuesdays, or Fridays. The answer to that is that you should stick to the plan. I tell my traders to avoid trading right after a big announcement. Why? Because there's too much flux in the market. Too many people are reacting with knee-jerk trades that inject too much emotion in the market. Waiting a day or two to let the market shake off this kind of volatility is better than investing in a whirlwind.

So, when it comes to when you should actually trade and act on your investing plans, Wednesdays and Thursdays often can be the best days. Experience will help you determine which days are best for you.

### Get Ahead of the Money

Monitoring reports and information is a crucial part of doing your due diligence and preparing to trade. Quarterly earnings reports are among those bits of information that investors typically follow. Quarters—and by that I mean quarters of the year—also serve as good benchmarks for assessing your strategy and making sure you are adhering to your plan. The challenge, though, is to avoid following the money. Instead, investors should get ahead of the money.

What do I mean by that? The end of a quarter is a not a good time to be following trends—either up or down. Generally what happens at the end of a quarter is that institutional investors—for example, big mutual funds that buy and sell in 100,000-share blocs—try to get laggards off the books. Although, of course, you want to make sure you're not holding on to duds that are doing your portfolio no good, the real key is to try to make sure that you're investing in leaders in the first place.

In fact, this is an advantage individual investors have over professional traders or institutional investors. Professionals need to make sure their investments look good on the books and on quarterly reports. They need to get the highest returns and the best possible results for their investments so it looks good on paper. Professionals call this "marking the books."

Individual investors, however, do not need to make decisions at the end of each quarter in order to mark the books. Instead, they need to be careful entering positions that have been strong during a given quarter so that they are not manipulated by "window dressing." Window dressing takes the form of artificially high prices—prices that have become distorted by end-of-quarter shenanigans to mark the books. Back in the old days, before electronic trading was widespread, savvy traders would fly back from vacation on December 29 and then fly right out after the close on December 31 to rejoin their families on vacation. The reason? Traders knew big hedge funds would be dumping losers and buying winners in a last-ditch effort to gussy up their performance for the year, so there was a lot of money to be made by riding these currents coursing through the trading pits on the NYMEX or the Chicago Board of Trade.

One thing investors can do to avoid window dressing is to shift time frames to create their own quarters. Normally, people look at a calendar and say that first quarter is January 1–March 31, second quarter is April 1–June 30, and so on. But I want you to move the quarters so that your first quarter begins after Martin

Luther King Day, making it roughly January 22–April 22. That's your new first quarter.

Why shift quarters? Because you're able to digest more information in those few weeks. If you're making an investment decision during this new first quarter, you're able to see a lot of capital flow in the market. You get to see how people are reacting to quarterly reports and earnings season (which begins around January 10). And you can avoid becoming part of the hot money that flows into the market on an annual basis at the beginning of the calendar year.

There are similar benefits for shifting your second quarter to April 22–July 21. One of those benefits is that that time frame allows you to get away from making important investing decisions around tax time (April 15). Instead, you're making your moves after tax season.

Your new third quarter, then, is going to be July 22–October 21. History shows that the weak period of the market usually is during the first couple weeks of October. If you just stick to the regular calendar, your normal fourth quarter would begin October 1—right when October typically starts getting dicey. If you shift your third quarter to mid-July to mid-October, you can better avoid making moves during what is historically a weak period.

Finally, your new fourth quarter becomes October 22–January 21. I like this a lot better because then you're not stopping cold at the end of the year. You're taking into consideration a little bit of the next year's price action. You're avoiding capital allocation flows that typically happen at the beginning of a calendar year. And, you're avoiding that period when fund managers are reallocating in order to make their statements look better.

In a way, this goes back to what we discussed in part I, which is determining a strategy and doing your due diligence. If you've done your homework and created an investing plan, you should not be easily swayed by the trends that appear in quarterly reports. Investors who are easily swayed are simply chasing money.

Instead, stick to your plan, do your homework, and stay ahead of the money by investing when it's right for you—and not when the talking heads or other self-professed experts say you should.

### Insert a Time Element to Your Trades

Most investors buy a stock with little thought of how long they want to hang on to that asset. In addition, few give more than a passing thought to exactly what kind of return they are looking for from any given investment. As a result, they—intentionally or unintentionally—subscribe to the buy-and-hold theory of investing, hanging on to assets come hell or high water. Few of us, though, can afford to be like Warren Buffett and hold a stock forever while it dips into negative territory and drags down the rest of our portfolios.

Before you invest in any asset, you first need to ask yourself how long you're willing to tie up your capital with it. How long are you going to tie up your investment capital before you decide to get out of a position? How long are you going to give an investment to pay off before you get rid of it?

I insert a time element into every trade. As mentioned in chapter 2, this gives me a gauge to determine whether I need to move on to another investment with more strength or momentum. Individual investors need to do the same thing. It is crucial to decide not only when to invest your money, but when to take profits and losses based on the goals you had for that investment going in. You make that decision based on your research and your understanding of what that investment can do for you—not just what you hope it will do for you. That requires you to look beyond headlines and bullet points into a fundamental understanding of the investment. You need to understand balance sheets and cash assets. You need to understand earnings reports and projections.

Here's the thing: you need to place a time stop on dead money. For example, I have talked a lot about the importance of reading quarterly reports. Why? Because by making that a regular practice, you can avoid being fooled, and as the saying goes, "Fool me once, shame on you; fool me twice, shame on me." Cisco recently put this old adage into focus.

On August 11, 2010, Cisco (CSCO) reported a bad quarter, and there was bad guidance after the close. The stock dropped to $21.42 (see figure 5.1). Any company can have a bad quarter, so an investor can be forgiven for letting that pass. But one bad quarter can be a sign of more bad things to come, and, at the very least, a bad earnings report should trigger you to keep note of the bad news and monitor what happens at the next earnings report.

On November 10, 2010, Cisco had another bad quarter with more bad guidance. The stock dropped from $24.49 to $20.46. It bumped back up a bit, but soon enough, it fell to $22.34, and it has yet to recover. As of June 2011, the stock was trading at $16.25.

This is why you need to read—and understand—earnings reports. You can overlook one bad quarter, but after that there are

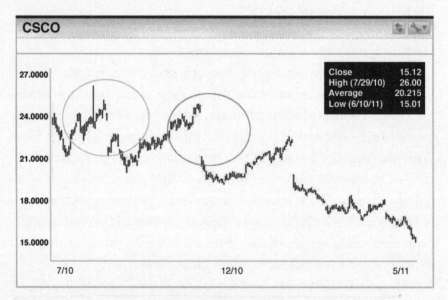

Figure 5.1: Cisco Price Chart, June 2010–June 2011

no excuses for holding a dying stock when the research doesn't back it up.

Based on your research, you need to set expectations and limits for your investments. That may mean you give an investment three months, four months, six months, to perform. Perhaps it's a year if that fits within the goals of your overall investment strategy. You should continually monitor your investments to determine whether each asset in your portfolio is doing what it needs to do. If it isn't, you need to jettison it. Your monthly calendar should include reminders to look not only at when to buy investments, but also when to reevaluate investments and possibly sell nonperforming assets.

Inserting a time element into trades is a simple best practice that seasoned professionals live by just about all the time. It helps take the emotion out of investing. It helps you avoid sitting on losers, which ties up your capital and makes it more difficult to invest in winners. Otherwise, you're holding a portfolio full of dead money.

## Determine the Value of Dead Money

Dead money is money that you have tied up in assets in your portfolio that aren't doing you any good. These are nonperforming assets. Dead money keeps you from investing in winners. The value of dead money is simple: you're allocating capital to an investment, and you're watching the weeds grow—while flowers are blossoming at the other end of the pasture. You're missing out on other opportunities. This is similar to what economists call "opportunity cost," which is the cost (that is, the price, benefit, or value) of selecting one thing in favor of another. The opportunity cost of parking money in nonperforming assets is that you don't have the free cash to invest in assets that are moving higher.

Let's use Microsoft as an example. In the introduction, we talked about the misperception that Microsoft is a great value stock. The fact is that Microsoft also provides a good example of dead money.

In January 2002, Microsoft was looking like a great company. A lot of investors got behind Microsoft after Bill Gates was held up as a model CEO whose genius had helped make him the wealthiest man on the planet. Most investors didn't give a thought to when they would get out of Microsoft; they just rushed in.

For the next seven years, Microsoft traded between about $20 and $35 (see figure 5.2). For Microsoft, that's a pretty narrow range. For much of the time, in fact, Microsoft traded between an even narrower range of $25 to $30. During the firm's accounting scandal of summer 2002, when Microsoft settled with the Securities and Exchange Commission regarding allegations of misrepresenting financial performance, the stock fell below $25. It would take until the final months of 2007 for Microsoft to trade above $35.

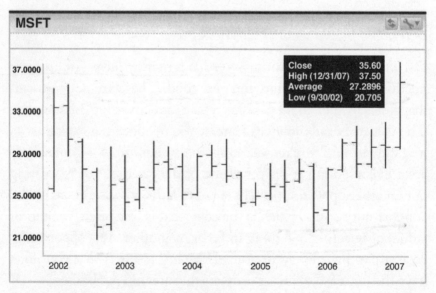

Figure 5.2: Microsoft Price Chart, 2002–07

Most investors rode that roller coaster and refused to get off despite the dips. But they should have been out of Microsoft based on the simple concept of return on capital. Investors should have known how much time they were willing to give that investment to earn a positive return for their portfolios. Instead of just jumping into Microsoft and hoping for the best, investors should have assessed Microsoft's prospects in light of their individual investing plans. They should have set solid expectations for what kind of return they wanted to get from Microsoft and for how long they were willing to wait to earn those returns. Instead, their investment turned into dead money—money they could have been using to pursue other, more profitable opportunities. Too many investors followed the herd and succumbed to hysteria—and got clobbered.

## Make the Most of Herds and Hysteria

I am, by far, not the first person to advise investors against avoiding herds. But even though "avoid herd investing" is a common investing tenet, it bears mention here. Why? Because with the pervasiveness of the Internet and the advent of electronic trading, it has become easier than ever to get caught up in the hysteria that oftentimes drives the markets. The herds have gotten bigger, faster, and nastier over the past decade. In 2001, the average daily volume on the S&P 500 was roughly 1.3 billion shares. By 2011, that had more than doubled to about 4.0 billion shares. The five largest one-day point gains and the five largest one-day point losses in the S&P 500 have all happened since 2000. More trades are coursing through the system as the herds pick up speed.

One of the challenges with avoiding herds is that too often we fail to recognize the noise of thundering hooves that are already surrounding us. We have, already, been caught up in the herd and hysteria. So how do you spot a herd so that you can actually avoid it? First you need to learn how to recognize the herd itself.

One of the clues that the herd is taking over is when investors, pundits, and so-called experts alike start saying things like "This time it will be different" or "The rules no longer apply" or other sweeping generalities that have no basis in the data. We saw that in the late 1990s when so many experts started calling for "Dow 36,000," which was a far cry from where the Dow was then—and now. We saw it in the early 2000s when investors rushed to buy tech stocks of companies with no balance sheets—just ahead of the dot-com crash. And we saw it more recently during the liquidity crisis when institutional investors fell in love with derivatives like mortgage-backed securities, even though they really didn't understand them.

One of the most foolhardy investments anyone can make is getting into a stock because an analyst has given it a significant upgrade. Just because a firm like Goldman Sachs adds Stock XYZ to its conviction buy list doesn't mean that an investor should rush out and buy that stock that very day. Instead, that signal should be considered a suggestion, an opportunity to put the stock on a watch list.

For example, when I see a stock land on a buy list, I make notes about both the asset itself and its sector—but I don't buy it that day. If my research shows me that the stock is a good one, if other factors like price and volume align, or if it looks as though the stock is showing signs of confidence, that's when I really look at buying it. It's not that I discount or disagree with the buy list recommendation; it's that I don't rush in right away. Only fools rush in, as they say. There's no reason to pull the trigger just because some talking head is urging the herd to stampede.

Herds and hysteria tend to go hand in hand with bubbles, all of which, of course, you want to avoid. Remember: a lot of what we've been talking about goes toward taking the emotion out of investing. Professional investors avoid herds and getting caught up in hysteria. These are some of the best practices that you can use to avoid them, too.

## Don't Get Caught Up in the Machine

Professional traders and individual investors alike can easily get caught up in the machine. What's the machine? By that, I mean that it's easy to get caught up in the ease of trading that has marked the advent of computers, electronic trading, and day trading. It's easy to get caught up in the nonstop blather of talking heads, pundits, gurus, and experts who are telling you twenty-four hours a day where you should be putting your money, what you should be buying, and when you should be selling.

When you're glued to your computer or television, watching prices fluctuate, it's easy to get caught up in the machine, especially when it comes to execution. All of this information—this noise—is right in front of you, practically begging you to do something about it. You're seeing dollars and cents, and you start to believe you could make some money on those incremental changes taking place every few minutes. You're seeing that you could buy Walmart (WMT) at $54.47. An hour later, it's at $54.87. You start to think that you could sell it and then buy it right back and make 40 cents a share. The next thing you know, you've thrown your investing plan out the window, you've forgotten to do your homework, and you've swept your investing team under the rug. You've gotten yourself caught up in the machine.

But it doesn't work. This kind of spontaneous trading—day trading, really—is probably one of the more unsuccessful strategies that most individual investors can participate in. Are there people out there who day-trade successfully? Sure there are. With day trading, nine times out of ten you could be right. But that one time that something happens in the middle of the day and you're wrong... you could lose it all. Most day traders are leveraging too much, risking too much, and losing too much.

I advise investors to avoid day trading. Nor should you be acting on every bit of information you glean from the Internet or television. Instead, take some time to do your homework, consult with your team, and determine whether that investment you just heard about is actually a fit with your annual investing plan.

## Don't Chase Hot Money

Just as it is too easy to get caught up in the machine, it's also easy to chase the hot money. By that, I mean those sexy, headline-grabbing assets that everyone is talking about—today. Chances are they won't be talking about those assets next month or next year. That's because hot money doesn't stay hot forever. Hot money usually is the first to fall, and it falls the hardest. Most investors have way too much of their portfolios invested in hot money.

Hot money could be a particular stock, fund, or commodity. For example, during the dot-com bubble of the early 2000s, a number of stocks soared and then crashed. Among them was InfoSpace. Founded in the 1990s by former Microsoft employee Naveen Jain at the start of the tech boom, the company went public in 1998. By March 2000, its stock had skyrocketed to $1,305 a share. But just over a year later, by April 2001, the stock had crashed to just $22 a share, a loss of about 98.3 percent of its value.

Bubbles often lead to crashes. Just as the tech bubble led to the dot-com crash, the housing bubble led to the liquidity crisis of 2008. Countrywide Financial was one of the victims of that crash and has since become the poster child for mismanagement and fraud. Countrywide launched in the early 1980s. By 2007, its stock price had gained nearly 25,000 percent. Though its climb into the stock market stratosphere by no means followed a straight line, Countrywide, for the most part, seemed to benefit from the home-buying frenzy that swept the nation. From a share price of about $2 in 1985, Countrywide's stock hit above $45 in 2007. Barely a year later, however, Countrywide was facing bankruptcy before it was bought by Bank of America.

There's a big difference between buying high and chasing the hot money. Buying high requires you to research quality assets that have solid data. Hot money, on the other hand, tends to be characterized by flimsy data fueled by rumor, speculation, and general hysteria. To understand the difference, let's look at gold. In December 2010, gold was trading as high as $1,429 an ounce— the highest it had been in decades (on an inflation-adjusted basis). There was no good reason for any investor to have sold gold during the previous ten months. But a lot of investors were forced to sell because they had chased the hot money and put way too much into gold. They allocated too large a percentage of their investing capital in what is, essentially, an expensive, sophisticated market. The price of gold has been soaring, up about $200 an ounce just since January 2010, as investors look to the precious metal as a hedge against the struggling economy. Gold has been making headlines for months. As a result, hordes of investors jumped into gold—in a big way and regardless of whether it fit their investing plans. Because they chased the hot money, most people are over-allocated in gold, forcing them to sell because their positions are too large.

Chasing the hot money leaves too many investors with dead money. That dead money leaves them little opportunity to invest in assets that are more suitable for their portfolios. By chasing the hot money, investors get caught up in the hysteria that drives markets—sometimes way up, sometimes way down. When they're chasing the hot money, most investors look only at price. They forget about doing their homework, studying the fundamentals, and sticking to their plan. And most investors aren't looking at volume, which also is important when it comes to avoiding herds and hysteria.

## Watch Volume as Closely as Price Action

When most people talk about their investments, they usually talk about what price they paid. They say things like "I bought Apple a year ago at $188, and now it's trading at $320." Investors rarely say, "I bought Apple while it was trading 15 million shares every ten days." But professional traders know that it is important to keep an eye on volume as well as price, because the two should be in sync.

Volume is the number of shares, bonds, or contracts traded during a given period. It can be measured for a specific security or for an entire exchange. Just like price, volume can be an indication of the mood of the market or of an individual asset. Volume also can provide investors with a sense of prevailing trends.

Let's say you're holding Google (GOOG) in your portfolio and that Google is in a significant uptrend, meaning price is increasing. But price isn't the only measure of the direction of an asset. When you're doing your homework on an asset that could be a fit for your portfolio, you also should be looking closely at volume.

Volume can be measured hourly, daily, weekly, monthly, yearly, or by any number of increments. The average volume I like to use is the past 30 days (but 90 days is also an acceptable measure and may be easier to identify). Let's say that Google provides some kind of indicator that advances the stock price higher. Perhaps it's going to launch a new platform or product. Maybe it announces better-than-expected earnings. Concurrent with the price increase, I also would expect to see a significant amount of volume come in to the stock (see figure 5.3). That increased volume is a sign that the news is generating a lot of excitement, which means that more investors are buying and selling the stock, which, in turn, increases its volume and helps move the price higher. (Investors can find volume charts online at such sites as bigcharts.marketwatch.com.)

The key is that the spike in volume has to match the spike in price action. So you need to make sure that volume is in sync with price action.

When price and volume are advancing in tandem, it can be a sign of a positive trend—and it can signal a potential buy opportunity. If you have a stock that gets positive news, the stock is in

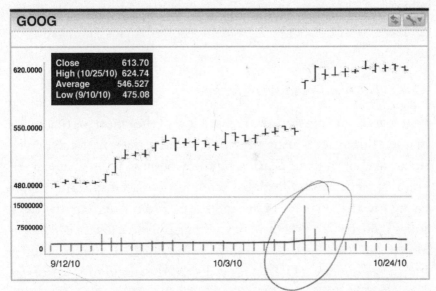

Figure 5.3: Google 30-Day Price & Volume Chart (any 30-day period)

an uptrend and it advances on positive news and positive volume. It's seen as a bullish indicator. Conversely, falling prices with high volume may be an indication that it's time to sell (a bearish indicator). It's also usually a bearish indicator if prices are rising but volume is falling. Traders don't like to see price and volume moving out of sync with one another. It could be a sign of trend weakness. Traders might, then, say that the trend "lacks commitment." So when price and volume are not moving in tandem on a particular investment, investors should take that as a sign to reevaluate their positions, especially if they are nearing the time limits they set for that particular asset to perform.

Although price is important, obviously it's not the only factor to consider when evaluating an investment opportunity. You have to do your homework. Professional traders know that keeping an eye on volume, especially as it relates to price, can help them determine whether buy or sell signals are evident. Monitoring volume is yet another best practice that can help investors take the emotion out of investing so that it becomes easier to buy high and sell higher. Because emotions—like fear and greed—often rule the markets.

## Make Fear and Greed Work for You

Fear, panic, and pessimism are just a few of the emotions that make markets fluctuate. During the past few years, these particular emotions have had a lot of bearing on the economy. I don't have to tell you that since 2008, the global economy has been suffering; sputtering toward recovery in fits and starts. From a high on the Dow Jones Industrials of 14198.10 in October 2007 to a low of 6469.95 in March 2009 and back up to 12,876 in May of 2011, the Dow Jones Industrial Average (DJIA) has reflected the mood of investors as they grapple with the struggling economy. Many investors have embraced the pessimism that has roiled the markets. A lot of investors have gotten out of the markets, and a lot of cash is sitting on the sidelines.

When investors gravitate toward the end of the spectrum that is characterized by complete and utter fear, opportunities arise. As we have discussed, when investors are fearful, it's time to be greedy. Fear is evident when cash is being raised. For instance, you might notice a spike in money market or T-bill holdings. That could be a great time to put new money in the market, because that could mean that pessimism has helped the market to reach bottom. That in turn means there are opportunities. There is an old investing axiom that says, "Buy when there is blood in the streets." Any time when the markets are marked by extreme fear or greed is a classic investing opportunity.

Opportunities come in many forms. It could be a great buying opportunity—a chance to invest in a good asset at a great price, which can be a credible form of value investing. It also can be a great chance to buy high and sell higher. And, although a lot of investors think only about buying opportunities when they think about capitalizing on fear and greed, they also should think about selling opportunities—about those opportunities to sell high and take profits.

For example, let's look at fall 2008, when the markets really started to collapse. As we mentioned, in October 2007, the Dow topped 14,000, setting a record. Over the next year, the Dow was up and down—though mostly down, sliding to 11,100 in July 2008 before plummeting to 8,451 in October 2008 (see figure 5.4). We now know that a perfect storm had hit, with the subprime mortgage crisis, the liquidity crisis, and a growing unemployment rate combining to form the Great Recession.

A lot of people look back at fall 2008 and say, "I got stuck. I couldn't get out." But there were plenty of opportunities to get out of the market before it tanked—plenty of opportunities to sell high. A number of telltale signs were present, indicating to investors that the markets were about to crumble.

For instance, remember earlier when I described our conversations at MBF about Visa and MasterCard. We identified that a monumental change was coming in the markets. The hedge fund

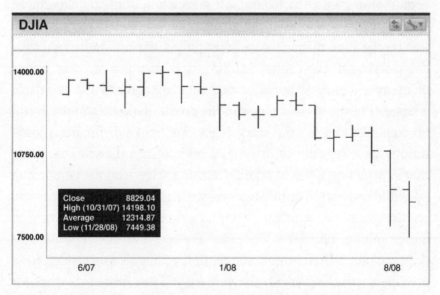

Figure 5.4: Dow Jones Industrial Average, June 2007–December 2008

crisis at Bear Stearns in July 2007 was leading to other signs that the market was in trouble. By late 2007, financial journalists and commentators were pointing out danger signs such as increased inflation, maxed-out credit cards and home equity loans, and growing debt, as well as uncertainty and volatility in the markets.

By October 2008, following passage of the Troubled Assets Relief Program (TARP), hedge fund and institutional money managers used the ensuing relief rally in the first two weeks of October to exit the market. They were selling high when they could, taking profits, and moving to the sidelines. I couldn't even tell you how many conversations I had with hedge fund and institutional money managers in the weeks that followed about how they were on the sidelines. Hedge funds, for example, liquidated way in advance of everyone else. In fact, a record number of hedge funds liquidated. Hedge Fund Research Inc. reported that more than 775 hedge funds liquidated in the fourth quarter of 2008, reflecting investor withdrawals of more than $150 billion. They avoided the collapse that came in the fourth quarter of 2008 and the first quarter of 2009. But I don't think most retail investors really began selling with any formidable conviction until late November 2008—nearly a year after the professionals moved to the sidelines.

Hedge fund managers are among the smartest intellectual capital working in the capital markets, and they got out way ahead of everyone else. Why? Because they recognized the winds of change. They saw the change in the credit markets, and the credit markets were telling the story (very few banks or financial institutions were lending to anyone, a telltale sign that the economy was contracting). They could see that jobless claims were going up while orders for durable goods were going down. They could see that corporate guidance on quarterly earnings was shifting to more ominous outlooks. They saw the fear that was brewing, and they got out. While others were suffering huge losses, hedge fund managers were breathing relatively easy. They made fear work for them.

Hedge funds were ahead of the curve at the onset of the Great Recession. They recognized that investors were fearful, and they acted accordingly by getting out of the market and selling high (or at least higher than most everyone else did). Individual investors can—and should—do the same. By not getting caught up in the machine and not chasing hot money, investors can avoid putting their money in investments that aren't suitable in the first place. By watching volume and price action, investors can gauge sentiment and see the directions in which assets and the markets are trending. By doing their homework, investors can see when others are becoming fearful and recognize the signs that the markets may be shifting.

Such shifts may well be indications that investing opportunities exist and that it's time to become greedy. But that doesn't mean investors should jump at every opportunity that presents itself. It also is important to have a diversified portfolio.

## Make the Most of Diversification

Everyone has heard the old adage "Don't put all your eggs in one basket," but diversification is one of the core tenets of portfolio management that average investors often misunderstand or fail to implement. A typical pitfall that mutual fund investors fall into is that they confuse having the right mix of stocks and bonds with being diversified. If these investors took the time to go through the top ten stocks in their personal funds and the mutual funds offered in their 401(k) plans at work, they would probably discover a fair amount of duplication. Unwittingly, they may have a large position in JP Morgan Chase or ConocoPhillips or some other stock that is a darling of fund managers.

Though some of the best professional traders are able to profit from just a few key holdings, most investors will do better to invest in a variety of themes and sectors. In the next chapter, we'll look at a trader who has succeeded by focusing on a few sizable positions—a focus that many experts would say isn't diversified enough. For most investors, though, it can be risky to allow just one or two assets to dominate your portfolio. Instead, diversification typically is a better way to go, at least when you're just on your way to becoming a more active investor.

Diversification means more than just splitting your portfolio between stocks in different sectors, though that is, of course, important. It also means that investors need to avoid glomming on to any specific theme. Investors also need to diversify by being active investors and by establishing limits. We'll look at those aspects of diversification in the next few pages.

### Avoid Overattraction to Themes

Diversification is important. It's especially important when the market is full of abnormalities, is acting erratically, or is suffering through an economic downturn. So what does *diversification* really mean? Well, it does mean making sure that you have a good mix of assets in your portfolio (e.g., stocks, bonds, and commodities). But it also means that you have to include a variety of stocks. Your stock holdings should include assets from different sectors. It should include small-cap, mid-cap, and large-cap investments. But diversification also applies to themes.

Let me explain what I mean by diversification when it comes to themes. Oftentimes, investors will approach me and say something like "I'm long some energy. I'm invested in copper and gold. And I've got some materials in my portfolio. What do you think?" I'll tell them that in essence, they're bullish on China. Why would I say that? Because most of those holdings show a bullish trend and stand to benefit from what's going on in China these days, which is showing a huge demand for energy, metals, and natural resources. The problem with having a China Bull Portfolio is that if China falls, so do the investments that correlate with China's economy.

Although China is interesting and there are some investing

possibilities there, the point I'm making really isn't about what an investor should do if China tanks. The point is that investors need to be diversified. You have to look at your holdings (*all* your holdings) to ensure that your portfolio (your *entire* portfolio) is balanced and diversified. Don't tell me that you're holding shares of Apple (APPL), Microsoft (MSFT), Google (GOOG), and maybe the Fidelity Select Software & Comp Fund (FSCFX) and then tell me you're diversified when each of those investments is basically in technology.

For a lot of investors, it's easy to fall in love with a theme or a sector and then start chasing the hot money within that theme. Whether it's technology or energy or China or whatever, it's important not to become overly attracted to a particular sector or a particular event. For instance, during the second quarter of 2008, everyone was caught up in an antidollar sentiment. Commodities became the hot money, and everyone was talking about it. In fact, one Friday afternoon, I was sitting in the waiting room of my doctor's office, watching television along with other patients and staff. CNBC was on. At one point, a nurse stopped to watch and listen to what the commentators were saying about oil. I couldn't help but notice her interest, so I said, "Are you long oil?" She turned and looked at me. And then she said, "Of course. Isn't everyone?"

Here's the thing: if everyone is talking about the soaring price of oil, you want to be careful about buying oil, investing in commodity ETFs that are heavily weighted in oil, and investing in companies whose main business is related to oil. Why? Because if oil falls, then each of your oil-related assets will fall as well.

The lesson for individual investors is to be diversified not just at moments of peril, but to be diversified at all times so that when the moment of peril comes, your portfolio is balanced enough to weather the storm. If your portfolio is balanced and diversified, you should not be forced into a position where you are required to sell your holdings.

A lot of investors make the mistake of looking for a particular asset to serve as a hedge to balance their portfolios. They want to know about specific investments that can help them stay diversified in case, for instance, China falls. But it's not a matter of which particular assets you should hold to provide diversification or a hedge against the fall of China. What investors should do is a paper-and-pencil analysis in order to understand their revenue exposure to China. Investors should ask what percentage of revenues are derived from China in a given company or asset, regardless of whether the company itself is based in China. It's not about holding particular assets in case China collapses. Diversification comes when investors are certain that too much revenue isn't coming from China alone.

Diversification provides a cushion and a little comfort to step back and say, "Okay. Now, strategically, tactically, what are we going to move here? How are we going to shift the chips? Do we want to go to cash?" Asking those questions requires you to examine how balanced your portfolio is and to actively participate in the success of your investments.

## Be an Active Investor

I've heard some so-called experts say that investors shouldn't bother looking at their quarterly statements; that they don't need to examine their holdings any more frequently than once a year. That's ridiculous.

You should be looking at your quarterly statements. If you aren't looking at them and reassessing your positions based on those statements, then you don't belong in today's market. You have to be an active investor if you want to enjoy any measure of success.

On the other hand, if you feel the need to be checking market activity several times during the day, then you likely are over-allocated. You might have too much going on. You might be too diversified. If you're worried over the weekend how your positions are doing, you likely have too much money in your positions. You need to be an active investor in order to survive in today's markets, but you also need to be able to walk away from each trading day without too much concern about what's going on with your holdings.

Passivity is the enemy of the individual investor. You've got to fight and work a lot harder these days to get the extra returns that you could get easily in years past. That means being more active, more tactical in your approach to the market. It means you have to assess your investing strategy, do your homework, keep diversified, and adjust your weightings accordingly. You have to keep your eye on your holdings to determine whether each of them is working toward your investing goals. This may well require you to adjust your holdings periodically. And if you aren't looking at your quarterly statements, you likely will not be in a position to adjust your holdings when they are no longer working for you.

Part of being a more active investor requires you to think in a more tactical way. Look at your bottom line. Cut costs where you need to. In the same way a corporation that needs to cut costs will fire workers who fail to produce and sell off divisions that are underperforming, you need to look at your portfolio every so often and sell your losers. The bottom line in your portfolio is your losers. We are no longer in an investing environment where anyone can afford to sit on losing assets and take sizable losses, hoping for better performance. Therefore, you have to focus on minimizing your losses, and that means you have to be more aggressive, you have to take a more active role in administering your portfolio than you're probably used to. You wouldn't put up with poor performance from an employee, so why would you be any more lenient with a stock?

Neither passive investing nor loading up on index funds is going to help you get that extra alpha that you want. Instead, think of your portfolio as your own index. Your index isn't going to look like anyone else's. You need to establish your own limits.

*Establish Limits*

Being an active investor doesn't mean you have to turn into a day trader who's watching every move the market makes every minute of every day. You do, though, need to monitor your holdings and make sure that your investments are working for you. If you think of your portfolio as your own index, you can customize your assets to suit your investing needs.

Your portfolio—your index—should be comprised of assets you want to include, not assets that some talking head says you should include. There is no reason to get caught up in the machine when you're building your index. Instead, you need to set your own parameters and establish your own limits.

Remember: it's your money. If you lose it, you're not getting a bailout. So you might as well invest your money in things you believe are important. It's okay to lose money—as long as you lose it investing in something you believe in. Don't lose it by following someone else's ideas.

What goes into your index? That depends on who you are as an investor. It depends on whether you're conservative or aggressive. Since you're using your money, you have the luxury of tailoring your index to your personality.

Consider your strengths and weaknesses and use that as a foundation. For example, I know that my strength is having an understanding above all else of the global macro environment. I understand the big picture very well. I understand energy. And I also recognize when momentum changes in a market. My index reflects my skill set as an investor.

For example, in early 2011, energy exposure remained the one area where I would have gone overweight (that is, added to my positions). Why? Rebellion and revolution in Africa and the Middle East were moving the markets. Global demand for energy was rising, and the risk of contagion in North Africa and the Middle East shined a spotlight on limited global energy capacity.

The oil market was aggressively adjusting pricing for supply disruptions in Libya and beyond. Understanding how these global events affected the macro elements of my investing plan allowed me to make the necessary adjustments.

Understanding macro events may not be your forte. Each individual investor is going to have his or her own index. There is no template. I can't tell you what you should include in your index (other than to say that it should be well diversified!). But I can tell you what shouldn't be in your index—and that is anything you don't understand. If you don't understand soy futures, then don't invest in them. If you really don't understand financial derivatives, then stay away from them. Investing in things you don't understand is a recipe for disaster. Warren Buffett is the poster child for this investment tenet: he avoids investing in technology-related stocks because he believes he doesn't understand technology.

What's important to understand is that just because you hear someone talking about an investing idea you don't initially comprehend, it does not mean that it is off-limits for you. Instead, make a note about the idea, do your homework, and see if it fits your investing strategy. If someone comes up to you and starts talking about cloud computing and how you could make a killing by investing in cloud computing, and you don't know what cloud computing is, then don't invest in cloud computing. It's okay not to know.

Let's say that you're a nuts-and-bolts kind of investor and you understand basic slow-paying dividend companies like Coca-Cola (KO) and Procter & Gamble (PG). Then that's your strength, so to speak. Make dividend-paying companies like these a core component of your personal index. That's what you've got to stay in. You need to set limits and stay inside your comfort zone when you're building your index.

Establishing limits isn't just restricted to the types of assets you will include in your index. You also have to look at the amount of holdings that you can have. As mentioned in chapter 2, I recommend somewhere between nine and twenty-two individual assets. That's about as many as most people can realistically keep track of. You'll find the right number for you, but you'll probably want to start out smaller and build up as you gain confidence.

You also need to establish limits regarding actual dollars and cents. How much money are you willing to invest in your overall portfolio? How much will you allocate to stocks? To bonds? How much will you leave in cash? Once you know how much you're willing to invest overall, you need to think about how much money you want to dedicate to each individual asset.

Whatever limits you set and however you establish the parameters of your portfolio, your limits will be, in part, dictated by your diversification plan. Diversification and limits work together, but you have to be actively engaged in your own plan. No one else is going to monitor your investments with the same interest that you will. Although your team will be there to help you, you're the only one who can pull the trigger. Knowing when to enter and exit the market will help you do that, and we'll look at that next.

# 6

# Know When to Enter and Exit the Market

Investors need to think about their trades in terms of both price and timing. However, timing is the factor that most individual investors routinely ignore. But when you enter and exit the market can mean the difference between success and failure. So in this chapter we'll take a look at four techniques that will help you master timing: appointment investing, maximizing winners, minimizing losers, and creating an investment calendar.

Most investors trade with only one price in mind: the amount they're willing to pay for an asset. In reality, though, that's a naïve way to approach an investment. Instead, investors should consider four price points: a buy price, a stop loss price, a price at which you start taking some money off the trade, and a price at which you start adding to a winner. We'll look at these later in the chapter when we talk about ways to minimize losses.

But let's start with timing and, more specifically, appointment investing. You may be familiar with the term *dollar cost averaging,* which essentially is buying securities at fixed intervals. Most people do this through automatic investments that are zapped out of their paychecks or bank accounts to their mutual funds or their 401(k)s, but few investors dollar cost average when buying stocks. Investors should dollar cost average with their stocks as well, especially when the price of that stock is appreciating in value. That's buying high and selling higher, which I contend is a far better investing strategy than "averaging down," which is what most investors do. Rather than dollar cost averaging, I like to call this method "appointment investing."

## Entering the Market through Appointment Investing

Most individual investors enter and exit the market in ways that do not help them maximize winners and minimize losers. In talking with many money managers and retail investors, it became clear to me that when an investor wants to own 400 shares of a stock, say JP Morgan Chase (JPM), he typically buys all the shares at once. That may seem easy and logical on some level, but it's usually a mistake.

Instead, I recommend that investors buy shares over time. It is not the length of time or the intervals that matter most, just the fact that one is averaging out the cost of those shares. Making an appointment—or several appointments—to invest in the market is often called dollar cost averaging. I prefer to call it appointment investing for three reasons:

1. Although some investors use dollar cost averaging effectively with mutual funds, very few investors use the technique with equities, and that is usually a mistake.

2. Appointment investing allows investors to take advantage of market weaknesses, which in some instances allows them to buy a security at a lower average price.

3. Some investors might confuse dollar cost averaging with averaging down, a very different investing technique with very different outcomes.

*Averaging down* has a very different meaning than *dollar cost averaging*. Averaging down means buying an asset repeatedly while the price of that asset is falling. For example, let's say you buy 25 shares of Priceline (PCLN) at $440. Then the price falls to $430 and you buy another 25 shares. You figure the price has to rebound. However, it continues to fall and reaches $420, and you buy it again, and then you buy it once more at $410. This is one of the worst investing concepts because you are not buying confidence. Instead, you are buying weakness. It might be okay to buy the stock once more after it fell to $430, but that's when you have to stop buying. If you don't, you are simply making the same mistake again and again and not protecting your downside.

Appointment investing is far superior to averaging down as well as to buying blocks of shares all at once. As mentioned above, appointment investing means buying an asset on regularly scheduled intervals regardless of the price of that asset. I want investors to get in the habit of buying stocks and other securities on an appointment basis. Perhaps you and your spouse designate every Saturday night as date night. I want you to purchase stocks in a similar fashion.

Why is this a superior method for entering the market? Because we are human beings, and our emotions often cloud our decision making; as a result, we are most likely to be wrong when we make an emotion-based decision to enter the stock market. Buying stocks on appointment over a period of time makes the process more objective and improves your chance of success.

So, going back to the Priceline example, you might decide to buy 25 shares every week on a Thursday just before the close, regardless of price. This technique works well in a market that is appreciating in value. In that scenario, you might pay more for each 25 shares, but you are adding to a winner, meaning that you are buying while confidence in that stock is building. Most people do not add to their winning stock positions, and I think that is a mistake and a lost opportunity.

If we look at the opposite scenario, when a market is falling, you are given the opportunity to buy shares at lower prices. But remember, you are buying those shares on a predesignated time no

matter what, regardless of price. You have a plan and you are sticking with it. Again, that's the difference between dollar cost averaging and averaging down.

To illustrate the point, let's return to the JP Morgan Chase
example we mentioned at the start of the chapter. An investor who
wants to buy 400 shares of JPM can be a smarter investor by using
appointment investing. Instead of buying 400 shares all at once,
this investor is going to buy it over time. Let's say he decides to buy
that stock every Friday just before the close (trading just before the
close ensures that he won't be exposed to nasty surprises late in the
trading day) for four consecutive weeks starting on the first Friday
in November. (As you've read previously, Friday is not my favorite
day of the week to enter the market, but let's assume that is the day
he chose because Thanksgiving would have gotten in the way of
buying on every Thursday that month.)

On that first Friday, November 5, 2010, JPM traded within
a range just above $40 and just below $41.50, and it closed near
$41, which is where our investor bought the first 100 shares of
what would become a 400-share investment (that was the highest
close of the month). The next Friday, he bought the second batch
of 100 shares into the close at $39.60. The third week, he bought
JP Morgan at $39.50, and on the last week, he bought the last 100
shares on the day after Thanksgiving at just around $37.60.

If he had bought the 400 shares over that four-week period
rather than all at once on the first Friday of the month, he would
have paid an average of $39.42 over those four weeks and saved
himself a total of 3.8 percent. That is a significant amount (roughly
$632 in this example).

Of course, you may ask, what if the price of the stock had been
rising throughout the month rather than falling? Then our investor would have paid more for the shares, right? In fact, in this case,
if he had bought all 400 shares of JPM on November 26, he would
have paid $37.60 a share instead of an average of $39.42 a share
(a difference of 4.7 percent or $728).

But hindsight is 20/20, and it's nearly impossible to time the market. The truth is that in most cases, appointment investing saves investors money over time. Some securities fluctuate wildly within any given week, which means that it is possible that price action on some Fridays may be down from the rest of the week. However, even if you paid a higher price each week, you would be buying an asset that is building on confidence, which we already stated is a winning strategy going in. Let's look at figure 6.1 to see what happened with the price of JP Morgan's shares.

Appointment investing does more than save investors money, though. It's also a good way to become more educated about your investments. By keeping those appointments with the market, chances are good that you get a better sense of how a stock is trading than you would have if you had bought all the shares at one time. Appointment investing forces investors to become more disciplined and attuned to the market, two factors that can help you achieve investing success.

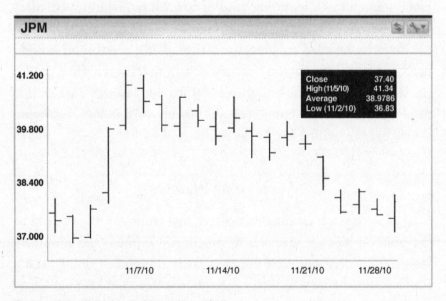

Figure 6.1: JP Morgan, November 2010

There are other advantages to appointment investing as well. One of the other benefits of buying shares according to a set plan is that if things don't go your way, you can always blame the plan versus blaming yourself. Let's say that over the course of a few weeks, you buy a stock that rises by 15 percent during the month. In this scenario, let's assume you end up paying 11 percent more than you would have if had you bought the shares all at once at the beginning of the month. By the last week of the month, you're kicking yourself. Had you only bought the shares all at once, you tell yourself, then you would have "earned" 11 percent in profit. However, it wasn't your fault. You had a specific blueprint for how you were going to buy those shares and, as such, you can more easily rationalize the "loss."

This may seem to fly in the face of appointment investing, but it really doesn't. Let me explain why. Sticking to your investing appointments allows you to forgive and forget more easily, since it was the plan that caused you to enter that trade at a higher price (and forgiving and forgetting are important traits of winning investors). Besides, you can congratulate yourself for identifying and buying a stock with that kind of upward momentum. Chances are, as we have discussed throughout the book, that the stock will continue its upward trajectory, so that even though you bought high, you have a very good chance of selling it even higher. And if the stock falls after you bought all 400 shares, you will now be able to identify reference points (e.g., a 50-day or a 200-day moving average) upon which to exit the trade.

## Maximizing Winners

One of my most fundamental rules of investing—which should be the goal of every trader—is to maximize winners and minimize losers. You may say, "Of course that is the goal. I don't need a Ph.D. to figure out that racking up big winners and keeping losses to a minimum will lead to investing success." Yet even though investors understand that rule on an intellectual level, most do not take the practical actions that will help them to achieve that all-important goal.

Let's use an example of an investor who is holding these four stocks: Pfizer (PFE), IBM, Netflix (NFLX), and Exxon Mobil (XOM).

This investor owns $15,000 worth of stock each for Pfizer, IBM, Netflix, and Exxon Mobil, for a total of $60,000. At the end of the quarter, he analyzes all of his holdings. Pfizer went nowhere, trading sideways for the entire quarter. Exxon was down a little, IBM was up a little. Netflix, however, was the big winner that quarter, with gains of 20 percent.

The investor understands how important it is to add to winners, so he adjusts his allocation accordingly. He understands strength and momentum, and decides to own $28,000 worth of Netflix at the expense of reducing his holdings in IBM, Pfizer, and Exxon Mobil so that his investments still total $60,000. He's going to maximize the winners and minimize the losers.

Who wouldn't do that? Doesn't that make sense? Institutional guys do it all the time. If buy low and sell high works, then why is it that in my twenty years of investing, I have seen the busiest markets when stocks were making new highs? It can't be that everyone is just selling. Someone has to be buying.

But that's only one side of the story. The busiest times in the markets occur at the extremes: on the up days when the market is showing the greatest strength and on those truly "Armageddon" days when traders are filled with fear and looking to sell everything in sight. But just because volume is high during market meltdowns does not take away from the argument that volume also is high on those most bullish of days, when stocks soar and make new highs. The key takeaway is that you can't be afraid to add to a winning position. Some of the greatest traders are those who know how to maximize their profits by buying additional shares of a stock or other security that is already working for them.

## Three Traders, Three Lessons

We can learn a few things from some great traders who aren't afraid of buying high and selling higher. When it comes to trading, I can think of a lot of traders who have taught me some important lessons. If I were putting together a Fantasy Trading Line-up, three traders I would want in the mix are Neil Rosenfeld, Evan Halpern, and Larry Altman. Each of these traders can teach a different lesson in how to maximize winners while buying high and selling higher.

Neil Rosenfeld is one of the greatest pit traders I have ever seen. He was by far the biggest independent oil trader on the NYMEX. What distinguished him from other traders? He had confidence and knew when he could go for the knockout punch, when he could go in for the kill. Neil was never afraid to buy on highs and then bid even higher. He knew how to maximize his winners. He did this even if he held a long position in whatever he was trading. It didn't matter to Neil. He would buy the highest offer and then bid above the highest offer without getting out of anything. That's what made Neil such a phenomenal pit trader: While those around him were cashing in winners, he was making even bigger winners without selling anything off.

Another great trader was someone named Evan Halpern. Evan, from the Five Towns of Long Island, was my first summer intern. He worked at MBF during summers when he wasn't attending the University of Maryland. Evan was a passionate trader and a passionate learner. He would be the first to arrive at the office and the last to leave. He was like a sponge and wanted to soak up as much information as he could about trading, talking to anyone and everyone he could, learning from more experienced traders.

Evan would trade short-dated natural gas contracts all the way out to long-term natural gas contracts. He was not just trading the spot price of natural gas. He was trading natural gas contracts that were deliverable three months from now, six months from now, eighteen months from now, and ten years from now. So he had multiple positions in the natural gas market. If you looked at all of those positions collectively, you could be rather certain that in terms of size Evan's largest position was what was working most for him. His most profitable position would be his biggest, which is the complete opposite of what most people do. Most people have a losing position as their biggest position. In order to create alpha, you must add to winning positions.

Remember that by *alpha* we mean returns that outperform industry benchmarks like the Dow Jones Industrial Average or the S&P 500. Once again, you should not do it all at once, but over some period of time that you determine in advance. Most academics and so-called investing experts would say that doubling down on potential winners is not a prudent way to invest and that you should keep your portfolio balanced at all times. But the reality is that this is how many professional investors make money. They do it by not being afraid to take a much larger risk than the investment textbooks recommend. However, the scenario I described is reality. The most confident investors are not afraid to go overweight to the extreme when all of the right indicators line up.

For example, a successful trader at Goldman Sachs or wherever who made $50,000 last week most likely did not earn $10,000 each day of the week. The probability is that he made $35,000 on Wednesday on his biggest holding. The best traders know this because they live it and observe this style of investing in their colleagues. I trade that way: it's when I trade best, in essence stepping on the gas pedal, maximizing winners, outsizing winning positions. Of course, I have been wrong about some of these outsized positions and lost money. That's why it is important to have tight stop loss orders on those large trades. (We'll talk about stop loss orders later in the chapter.)

But this all makes sense if you think about it: shouldn't you lose the most money on those investments that you have the most confidence in, even if it goes against you?

Another trader who epitomizes the "buy high, sell higher"

story is Larry Altman. Larry started out as a pit trader in the crude oil futures market back in the early 1990s. There are two things to know about Larry: He was one of the most emotionless traders I have ever seen, and he understood the need to change and evolve.

Whenever I walked into the pit, Larry would always ask me about my kids and my family. He would remain calm when the market was making new highs or new lows. And he would always say the same thing whenever I saw him: "How high is high? How low is low? Who knows the answer to that? Nobody." Larry had an uncanny ability to take emotion out of the situation even when everyone else around him could not. By keeping emotion in check, he was making analytical decisions based solely on what was happening in the market. By taking emotion out of the equation, he was able to ride his winners longer than most investors I have ever observed.

The other thing about Larry is that he was the perfect example of understanding the need to change as a trader. In the 1990s, he was a crude oil pit trader. But he was a forward-looking guy and recognized that the model for trading would change, that it would go beyond the floor to electronic trading. He was one of the first to make the switch to electronic trading, as early as the early 2000s. He evolved from being a crude oil pit trader to trading mini S&P futures. E-mini S&P contracts are one-fifth the size of standard S&P contracts. Professional traders utilize them because they offer deep liquidity and cost efficiency. In terms of volume, he's now probably one of the biggest mini S&P traders in the world, and he does it all from Aspen, Colorado.

Neil, Evan, and Larry are three great traders who know how and when to enter and exit the market to make the most of each investment. Neil Rosenfeld was the confident investor who did not care how high the market was trading—he would buy higher. Evan Halpern had a unique ability to maximize his winners: he would usually hold one position that would dwarf his other investments in size. Larry Altman had the ability to take emotion out of every trade, which also helped him to keep his winners longer than almost anyone. Each of these traders had his own unique strength, which helped him to maximize his winners and minimize losers. The key is to figure out what you do well so that you can mature, gain invaluable experience, and succeed on your own terms.

Before moving on, one word of caution: you cannot be a one-trick pony. That is, you can't just trade one part of the market, such as energy. You need to have at least a few investments that tend to work for you. For example, I always have some technology, I always have some energy, and I always have some commodities. In only the worst of times do I pare back completely in any of these areas (late 2008 after the fall of Lehman Brothers was the last time I did so). At times like that, I typically pare down to energy and commodities. I try to find the biggest and best balance sheets. That worked well for me in the case of Exxon Mobil (XOM), which became my energy play in fall 2008. You need to familiarize yourself with several sectors, securities, and commodities. If you don't, you will invariably miss an important opportunity when it comes along.

### Riding a Winner: Netflix

Let's take a look at the performance of Netflix during 2010, which is one more example of a "buy high, sell higher" winner. You could have bought Netflix at almost any time during 2010 and come out a big winner. And you could have added to the position almost any time and increased your winnings. Figure 6.2 tells the Netflix story. The Netflix story makes sense from almost every perspective. The fundamentals of the company were strong. In early 2009, the company hit the milestone number of 10 million customers. For only $7.99 per month, anyone can become a Netflix member, have movies delivered to his home in about one day, and watch as many streaming movies or TV shows as he wants (although not all Netflix movies are available for instant viewing). Netflix clearly is the category leader, and this leading mail-order DVD rental company has the kind of competitive advantage that most other companies dream about.

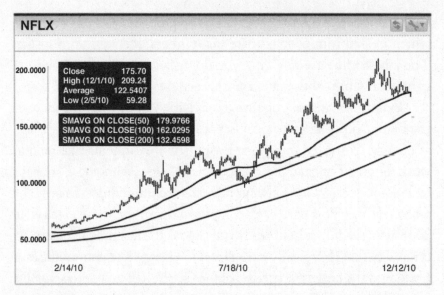

Figure 6.2: 1-Year Chart (2010) of Netflix, with the 50-, 100-, & 200-day moving averages

A few things may be going against Netflix's stock, however. In late 2010, the company was trading at about 70 times earnings, making the stock appear expensive when compared with the average stock (in most years, the average stock trades at about 15 to 20 times earnings). Another potential negative is that Netflix traded below its 50-day moving average three times throughout the year and one time violated its 100-day moving average. But it did that on low-volume days, and never once did Netflix fall below its 200-day moving average.

An institutional investor or trader might have used one of those instances to lighten up on Netflix by selling, say, a third or half of their shares during one of those instances. However, the best traders would have stayed with Netflix throughout the year, recognizing that the volume on those down days was light and not meaningful enough to warrant selling out the entire position. A professional investor also would note that the entire stock market was weak during those days on which Netflix violated one of its moving averages. However, even if a professional did sell some shares on one of those days, he might have decided to build back up the position once the stock traded safely above all three of its moving averages. This is a good trading scenario to study, because everything about Netflix was signaling strength. Figure 6.2 shows an orderly appreciation of the stock price throughout the year. Netflix was one of the biggest winners of 2010.

In mid-2011 the fundamentals of the company changed. Executives initiated a controversial new pricing program, which prompted subscriber defections and head-scratching on the Street. Instead of $9.99 for both DVD-by-mail and unlimited streaming services, the services were broken into separate plans ($9.99 for streaming, $7.99 for DVDs; or $15.98 for both). To many consumers, this felt like a stealth rate hike of 60 percent. The pricing plan change, as well as other factors, initiated a riotous price decline from $304 to $130. The sudden and severe drop is a yet another reminder of the dangers inherent in being a buy-and-hold investor in a volatile world, and it reinforces the importance of always being tactical, nimble, and vigilant.

## Minimizing Losses

Mark Fisher taught me a valuable lesson that to this day helps me minimize my losses: always use stop loss orders when entering the market. That is, always place two trades at one time: the entry price and the reference price point that we would use as a stop loss order. A stop loss order is a request to sell a certain number of shares when a security falls to a specified price, which is called the stop price. A stop loss order is like a safety valve. It's like a parachute that keeps you from dropping like a stone when down is the only direction things are headed.

Mark regularly used stop loss orders. At MBF, Mark would call me on the intercom and say, "Joe, buy me 10,000 IBM and put a stop in." It would be a price stop as well as a time stop, maybe $150 for 120 days. We also would discuss the point at which he would be willing to get out of the position. Mark was telling me to buy 10,000 shares of IBM and to put in the right reference point for a stop price. He trusted me to make that decision. Every trade we made was a two-decision trade: when to get in and when to get out. I can't remember one instance in which Mark would place a buy order without asking me to place the sell order at the same time. I recommend that all retail investors follow Mark's example.

In many instances, if you are watching the markets closely, you can weather a situation in which you don't have a stop by selling that security when it falls below one of your reference points—your mental stop loss order. However, even though you may be able to handle that four out of five times, it will be the fifth time—the day you're racing out the door to catch your kid's school play or you're getting a root canal or you went out to grab some lunch—that wipes everything out. I have seen years of gains vanish within a single trading day because someone did not have a stop loss order in and did not move quickly enough to liquidate a position. When equities started to roll over in March 2000, I remember us being stopped out dozens of times, being stopped out on Cisco, Microsoft, Intel, and the list goes on (*stopped out* means that our stop loss order point was violated). Mark would say, "Okay, we're stopped out." And I would say, "Okay, we move on." We wouldn't put the trade back on again (meaning we would avoid buying back any of the stocks we were stopped out on for a duration of weeks or months, in essence, putting that security in the "penalty box"). We took the stops in stride and then simply watched and waited. We did a good job of sitting on our hands and did not try to force a trade when markets were going the wrong way.

## Trailing Stop Loss Orders

The other key to using stop losses is to use what is called "trailing stop loss orders." Trailing stop loss orders are stop loss orders that are changed by the investor to protect a certain amount of profit or limit one's losses.

## Table 6.1: Share Prices and Trailing Stop Prices

| Share Price | Trailing Stop Price | Maximum Loss per Share | Maximum Trailing Loss per Share |
|---|---|---|---|
| $15.50 | $14.80 | $0.70 | $0.70 |
| $16.25 | $14.95 | $1.30 | $0.55 |
| $16.80 | $15.30 | $1.50 | $0.20 |

Here is how it would work: Mark would tell me to buy Intel up to $15.50 per share and put in a stop loss order price of $14.80. Once we bought the shares, the price of those shares rises to, say, $16.25. Mark would call me up and tell me to raise the stop. Set the stop at $14.95. Now the price of Intel goes to $16.80. Mark calls me up and tells me to raise the stop yet again, this time to $15.30. Now all we could lose on the trade is 20 cents (the difference between the $15.50 we originally paid and the new $15.30 stop price). In essence, what developed was a free trade (meaning that at worst we would either break even or lose only a few dollars), and there are few things that traders love more than a free trade. Let's take a look at table 6.1 to see these trailing stop loss orders once again and give you a clearer look at how they work (these stops are for illustration purposes and not exact reference points).

Most retail investors do not use trailing stop loss orders enough. If I asked ten individual investors if they use trailing stops, I am confident that no more than one would say he did. And that is a real problem, because a trailing stop loss order is one of the best defense mechanisms that an investor could use, and it doesn't cost a cent to place a stop and keep raising it as the price of the security rises. Trailing stops helped us a great deal back in 1998 and 1999, more than any time I can remember. The best traders instinctively use trailing stop loss orders because they have seen extreme volatility and understand the importance of protecting both their upside and their downside.

Trailing stops are used when the price of an asset is increasing in value. If, in the previous example, Intel, which we bought at $15.50, sinks to its original stop of $14.80, that's it: we're out. Intel goes into the penalty box for at least one quarter. Some investors do exactly the wrong thing by lowering their stop loss orders when their stock is falling. That is a major mistake made by novices who have not grasped the importance of preserving their capital. Lowering your trailing stop loss orders again and again defeats the purpose of placing the stops in the first place.

Here is what some investors do with their stop loss orders. Once again, using the Intel example, let's say an investor bought in at $15.50 with a stop loss order set at $14.80. When the stock falls to say, $15, they say to themselves, "I am not giving the stock enough room to climb, and I am going to get stopped out at $14.80." So that investor lowers the stop to $14.40, risking more money on that investment than he ever intended. He rationalizes lowering the stop because the last thing he wants to do is get stopped out and take a loss. This type of investing behavior is what undisciplined investors do all the time. Resist the urge to lower that stop when your stock is falling. You will only increase your losses and your frustration level. Remember that the key is to minimize losses and live to fight another day with as much of your investment capital in hand as possible.

## Investing by Season

Another factor that institutional investors take into account that individual investors do not is the seasonality of investing. Certain times of the year are more favorable for certain sectors than others. Seasonality is one of my favorite topics. Why? Because it has helped me make better investment decisions year in and year out. A year's worth of the crucial events that can affect the market is a lot of data points for any investor to keep in his head. That's why I find breaking a year into seasonal chunks helps to demystify the market and bring it into sharper focus.

## Technology Season

Let's start with the technology sector. Historically, technology tends to perform the best from about Labor Day to the beginning of December. That's the appreciation period. There are a couple reasons why technology tends to do well toward the end of the year. One reason has to do with technology's relationship to the U.S. dollar. As we discussed in previous chapters, leaders of most industrialized countries often crave a weaker dollar so that their goods and services are more attractive to overseas buyers (obviously they get more goods per dollar when their currency appreciates vis-à-vis the U.S. dollar). As the U.S. dollar weakens, it benefits technology because more than 54 percent of technology revenues are derived from outside the United States.

In addition, U.S. currency tends to be weaker in September and October and stronger in January and February. It doesn't really matter why currency is weaker or stronger at different times—it just is, and professional traders know to accept that. The statistics are there to prove the point. The bigger question is when a change in strength will occur, because it always does. For now, just know that from Labor Day to the beginning of December, institutional money managers tend to allocate capital toward technology. The lower dollar tends to hike the sales of technology products as overseas buyers take advantage of the favorable currency trade. It is the equivalent of U.S. technology products going on sale in non-U.S. countries. However, the currency side is only a part of the story. The other part of the story involves the holiday season.

Consumer technology products make great holiday presents. Who doesn't love a new gadget for Hanukkah or Christmas? Whether it is an iPad, a new laptop, or a Kindle, consumer technology is one of the most popular holiday presents. That's why stores like Radio Shack and Apple have a year-end push in order to maximize their sales. Many companies do as much as 30 percent of their business around Christmas, and technology tends to benefit more from that trend than other products (in 2010 alone, 212 million Americans shopped during Black Friday, the weekend after Thanksgiving).

There is a downside to the technology seasonality as well. There is vulnerability in the technology space that occurs at the beginning of the calendar year. That is when asset managers tend to sell off and cash in their technology winners. This pattern played out perfectly in 2009. During the last months of the year, there was what some professionals call a "melt-up" (an urgent buying in the market, or the opposite of a market crash) in the technology space (and the overall market) as money managers who were underperforming the S&P 500 played catch-up by buying into the big names in technology like Apple (which was up significantly in the year and topped $200 a share in December 2009) and Google (which was also way up for the year and topped $600 a share that same month). The reason this happened is that every money manager strives to beat the performance of the benchmark S&P 500 index, and they will risk a great deal of capital to make sure that their performance is better than the average S&P index fund.

What all this boils down to is that in August, I'm looking to move into technology. By April, I'm looking to have my holdings very low in this sector.

The energy sector experiences a seasonality similar to the technology sector. Energy tends to do well during the third and fourth quarters of the calendar year. However, energy offers one more key opportunity that is in direct contrast to the technology sector, and that is the first quarter of the year. During the first three months of the year, you have a good chance of succeeding in the market by buying refiners such as Holly Corp (HOC), Sunoco (SUN), Frontier (FTO), and Volero (VLO). What you hope to see during that first quarter is the profit margin of these refiners increasing, thereby raising the stock price of producers of gasoline and heating oil.

Once again, the time to own these refiners is ahead of the driving season, which comes during the second quarter around Memorial Day. You want to get in front of that, which means owning them in the first quarter. The vulnerability for these stocks comes in the second quarter, when the driving season arrives in May. The next opportunity to own these refiners comes in the third quarter, which is a quarter ahead of winter and the heating oil season.

Of course, none of these recommendations is an automatic buy. You need to do your due diligence to see if there is strength in each of the sectors before you invest, regardless of season.

## Commodity Season

There is seasonality to the commodities space as well. By *commodities*, I am talking about things like oil, natural gas, gold, and sugar. Commodities are things people need year-round, but they, too, have a seasonality component to them when it comes to investing.

I urge investors to avoid any significant allocations to commodities before Martin Luther King Day, which usually falls between January 16 and January 21. This is because during this period, many funds (including index funds, which are funds that are tracked to an index like the S&P 500) are allocating and reallocating to the commodity space.

For example, let's say you have an index fund that includes several commodities. In Year 1 of the fund, the exposure to commodities is 18 percent to oil, 11 percent to natural gas, 10 percent to gold, and 5 percent to sugar. Then in Year 2, the fund managers decide to reallocate. This reallocation means that they're going to have to buy certain commodities and sell certain commodities. They're rebalancing. The first three weeks of January is a rebalancing period for hundreds of funds, and they do it over a period of several weeks, so it's an orderly rebalancing. I believe that most investors—particularly retail investors—should stay out of the water when these big institutional tides are coursing through the commodities market as funds rebalance because of all of the uncertainty associated with the reallocation of commodity-based funds.

Here is a summary of how I recommend investors approach the commodity space from a seasonality perspective:

- Avoid being market weight or overweight to commodities during the first three weeks of January.
- Buy the refiners (stocks like HollyFrontier Corp and CVR Energy Inc.) in the first three months of the year.
- Assess oil and natural gas in the second quarter of the year and, if you see strength there, then consider taking a big position in these commodities.
- Look to own refiners in the third quarter, which is a quarter ahead of winter and the heating oil season.
- Look to be market weight or overweight energy during the third and fourth quarters of the year.

To recap, just like stocks have seasons, so do commodities. (We'll talk more about commodities in depth in chapter 9.) During the first three weeks of the year, you should not invest heavily in commodities or commodity funds—instead, you should look to own refiners. The second quarter is a good time to look at investing in actual oil and natural gas itself (rather than in the refiners). The reason is that the second quarter is a period during which market professionals are beginning to look forward and anticipate what the second half of the year's difference between demand and supply is going to be in the energy sector. So, if you look at this from a seasonality standpoint, there is more of an opportunity to identify confidence in the natural gas and oil markets in the second quarter. You should be assessing the overall strength of energy earlier in the year because that is the period that represents a potential bull market in energy (taking the aforementioned caveats into account, such as avoiding commodities for the first three weeks of the year).

## When to Avoid Putting New Money to Work

Just as there are good times and good ways to enter the market, there are times and ways that investors should avoid investing. Let's look at a few of them.

### Avoid New Quarters

We talked a bit about quarters in chapter 5. In addition to shifting quarters ahead by a few weeks, you'll remember that I recommend investors avoid doing any significant buying of stocks or commodities for the first few days of each quarter. Instead of putting money to work during those first few days, you should be closely observing what is going on in the market. That is because the first few days of a quarter often set the tone for the entire quarter. There often is a momentum change that takes place at the beginning of each quarter. Is the market performing well, or are we off by a few hundred points in the first ten days of the year? You want to use the calendar to your advantage to take the temperature of the market and get a good, up-close look at any meaningful shifts.

The beginning of a quarter is a pivotal time for the financial markets. That's because this is a natural point for the markets to change direction. I also believe that investors need to watch what happens on the fifteenth and thirtieth of every month. Millions of people get paid on those two days, and there is an automatic contribution to their 401(k) plans on those days. Once again, because investors do not know how funds are being allocated or reallocated, I recommend that investors do not aggressively invest on these days. The same holds true for the beginning and the end of every month. This may sound like market timing, but it really isn't. It is about not being lured into making significant investments because what appears to be a market surge is really a false opportunity.

However, there is one important exception to timing inflows to the market, and it takes place just one day a year, on March 15 (as long as that day falls on a weekday). The most highly compensated executives, C-level executives (CEOs, CFOs, etc.), and middle managers get their annual bonuses on March 15 (if it's a weekend, then they would get that pay the following Monday). One of the reasons I took a chance in early March 2009 by going overweight was that I wanted to get ahead of all of that executive compensation hitting the equity markets on March 15. Some people might say that I caught a falling knife. But it wasn't that. It was a combination of factors that prompted me to be confident about a market reversal, and all of that financial firepower hitting the markets was a part of that story.

### Avoid Investing When Europe Is Burning

When talking about getting into the market, investors also need to be aware of the relationship between the U.S. and European markets. In 2010, for example, there were many days that the European debt crises infected the U.S. markets. The inability of certain European nations to pay their debt started with a $100 billion problem in Greece and then spread to other nations including Belgium, Ireland, Italy, Portugal, and Spain. This led to uncertainty not only in the European markets but in the U.S. markets as well. And at times like that, when uncertainty and emotions are ruling the market, it's best to sit back and avoid entering a position.

It also is important to note that the European markets stay open until 11:30 a.m. Eastern Standard Time. When there is trouble brewing in Europe and the European markets are down, they will have their most profound effect on U.S. markets up to 11:30 a.m. EST. That's why I urge investors to take note of the European markets, and if they are down, stay away from putting new money in the market that day until after 11:30 in the morning. This way you reduce the chance that there will be additional nasty surprises that could sink any new investment due to events happening in the European markets.

## Avoid Midday Trading

I also do not like to trade in the middle of the day. If you look at the trading desk at a firm like UBS or on the floors of the major U.S. exchanges, you will find that those trading floors are less populated during the day than they are at the open and going into the close. There is less liquidity during the day, which simply means fewer people are trading and the price movement of the stocks might easily be reversed or exaggerated at the close. This is why, as stated earlier, I like to make appointments with the market, and when I do, I usually make that appointment to buy a security going into the close. Those are the times that the volume is heaviest and investors obviously get the clearest sense of how things will end up for that day. So if I decided in a given week that I was going to buy 800 shares of Apple, I may decide to buy 400 shares on Wednesday at 3:45 p.m. EST and the same number of shares at 3:45 p.m. on Thursday.

Some investors may wonder whether you can set an execution time on a brokerage order rather than an execution price. Online retail brokers should offer the ability to execute based on time, but they really don't. For instance, ideally an investor would be able to say that at 3:45 p.m. on Thursday, sell this or buy this. Institutions hire programmers to execute their trades like this and they write code to execute at specific times. Unfortunately, this is beyond the reach of most retail investors.

We talked about the beginning of the quarter—what about the beginning of the year? Should you be putting new money to work in January? This is an interesting question because the answer has changed over time.

## Is There a "January Effect"?

In the early 1990s, two top researchers[*] wrote a book entitled *The Incredible January Effect* (Dow Jones-Irwin, 1992). These two authors discussed a potentially very valuable phenomenon: for decades, certain stocks (lower-priced securities) tended to deliver "unaccountably high returns" during the month of January. That was likely due to the allocations that money managers and other financial professionals made in the first weeks of the year, after selling off losing stocks in December for the favorable tax benefits (to cancel out capital gains). However, like other similar phenomena such as these, after its discovery, the effect ceased to exist. Let's take a look at a few recent years to see if the January Effect still works:

• In 2008, the Dow opened around 12,000 and spent the rest of the year going straight down, achieving a 38 percent decline that year. The S&P was down a similar percentage: Every dollar put into an S&P 500 index fund that year was worth only 62 cents by year end (see figure 6.3).
• In 2009, the market rebounded from the 2008 lows. However, the Dow opened above 8,500 and in March hit a low of about 6,500. While the market rallied off that point, clearly January was not an optimal entry point in 2009 (see figure 6.4).
• In 2010, the Dow opened at around 10,400 but fell in January and part of February to a point just above 9,800. However, by March the markets were in rally mode (see figure 6.5).

What do we make of all of this information? First, I do not believe in the January Effect. It may have worked once, but since

---

[*]The two researchers/academicians were Robert A. Haugen and Josef Lakonishok. However, the first researcher who reportedly discovered the January Effect was a graduate student at the University of Chicago named Donald Keim. He had studied returns in the market from 1963 to 1979.

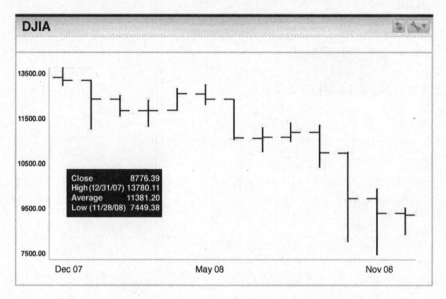

Figure 6.3: Dow Jones Industrial Average, January–December 2008

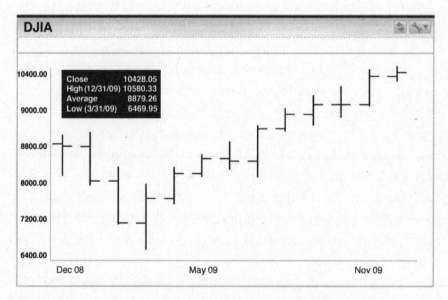

Figure 6.4: Dow Jones Industrial Average, January–December 2009

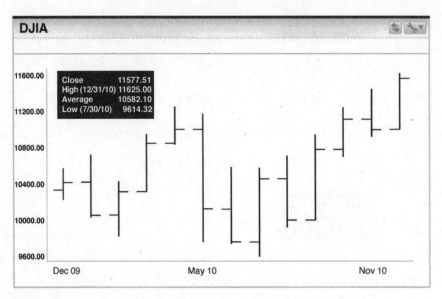

Figure 6.5: Dow Jones Industrial Average, January–December 2010

the liquidity crisis of 2008–09, putting new money to work in January could have led to significant losses, depending upon the year and an investor's time horizon. But in each of those years, there were better entry points than January.

Here is what I do, and I recommend all investors do the same. By now my penchant to observe the market rather than trade the market should be evident. I believe in going into January of each year, with my eyes open but my wallet shut, at either underweight or market weight. The year 2010 was no exception. In late February 2010, the market rallied back above its 50-, 100-, and 200-day moving averages. That told me to increase most of my positions to overweight by the beginning of March and stay overweight until early May, when once again the Dow slipped below all three of its key averages during the Flash Crash on May 6.

There is a saying in the investment world that says, "Sell in May and go away." I do not fully subscribe to that investing tenet, but I do agree with part of it. In 2010, I urged investors to move to underweight or market weight in May and then do nothing until

September, when once again confidence returned to the market and the Dow traded above all three of its key moving averages. I am not suggesting that investors make ten moves a year, but more like four to six moves a year depending upon what is happening in the market. The key is to monitor constantly all of the macro and micro events we discussed in part I of the book so that you know precisely when you should be making these kinds of adjustments to your holdings.

## Adjusting and Exiting

Selling in May might not always be sound investing advice, but knowing when to get out of (or reduce) a position is one of the most important—and the most difficult—things for individual investors to do. Most investors hang on to their investments for far too long, often watching their investments lose money and scrape bottom, but also often watching them profit, thinking those profits will continue into perpetuity. Neither approach is what I recommend.

Instead, there are a number of things individual investors can do to adjust their holdings and exit positions in order to achieve the "sell higher" portion of the "buy high, sell higher" strategy. We've already talked about some of these things, like adjusting losing positions and using stop loss orders and trailing stop loss orders. Let's take a look at a few more ways investors can exit positions.

### Set Upside Prices, Reference Points, and Time Elements

Most investors are impatient with their winners (they get out of those trades too quickly) and too patient with their losers (they sit on losing positions hoping for them to turn around). We don't sell soon enough because we ask, "What if I do sell now and I end up selling at the bottom? I could make more money if I wait a bit longer." In part, investors do that because it's just human nature. But investors also do that because they haven't set targets or reference points when they enter their positions.

Whenever an investor enters a position (that is, buys an asset), he should know what he wants that asset to do for him. He should have a profit target in mind. And, with that, he should have in mind a reference point for getting out of the position as well as a target price. He should know what his ultimate price target is, and he should know how long he's going to give that asset to get there.

If you've done your due diligence and you're ready to buy an asset, you should have a sense of the profit potential of that asset. You also should have a sense of how long it should take for the investment to reach that potential. If the investment fails to reach its target price within the prescribed time frame, you should sell—it's a loser—a nonperforming asset—and you don't need it sitting in your portfolio tying up your capital. You could invest instead in something more profitable, something that will be a better fit for your overall investing strategy.

## Sell Half

You always want to place yourself in a position where you maximize your winners. One of the ways to determine early on if you're potentially right or wrong about an investment is to measure how quickly it reaches the upside price target you set for it. What do you do if it hits that target sooner than you thought? What if it misses the target? Either way, you should be thinking about selling.

For example, let's say that you buy Best Buy (BBY) at $30 in April. Based on your research, you think that Best Buy should be trading at $35 by June 30. All of a sudden, though, it's trading at $35 by May. What do you do? You have a couple of options.

First, you could add to your position and raise your stop. Chances are there is something going on with Best Buy that requires you to be more aggressive about your investment. So, you should raise your point of reference bottom stop. You also should raise your upside price target.

Another option is to sell half or a third of your position, take your profits on that portion, and then set a new price target on the remaining shares. Why would you sell half the position? Because that allows you to lock in profits on at least a portion of the investment. Then, you can set a new upside price target, a new reference point, and a new timeline on the remaining position.

What do you do, though, if your investment fails to reach the price target within the time frame you allotted? You need to pull the trigger. If an investment is not working for you, if it isn't helping you reach your goals, then you need to get rid of it. If the share price is declining, then you should take your losses and chalk it up to experience. If the share price is increasing, but not at the rate you expected, you could, again, consider selling half of the position. Selling half protects your downside while still leaving yourself room to capitalize on some upside potential that may still be there. The key is to monitor the investment in order to make sure that it is still a fit with your investment strategy.

### Sell Before the Top

Selling an investment when it is climbing can be tough for a lot of investors, but it is something that professionals do all the time. Just as it's difficult for so many investors to sell a loser ("What if it comes back? I could recoup my losses."), it can be difficult to sell when a stock is surging ("What if I sell now and the stock still climbs? I would lose out on profits."). But professionals know that it's important to stick to your plan and monitor price targets, especially if the market is surging wildly.

Most people think of panics as crazy sell-offs where investors rush to get rid of their holdings before the bottom falls out. But panic buying can be just as crazy, with high volume often driving prices up to stratospheric levels that don't make any sense. That kind of frenetic buying often leads to indiscriminate investing—the kind of investing is too often driven by emotions. You want to avoid that kind of investing.

If you see that kind of frenetic investing, which often is marked by increased volume and explosive price action, you should consider selling because chances are that investment is about to peak. And the faster it peaks, the more likely it is that it will fall just as quickly. You want to get out before the asset plummets back to reality. You may lose some money on the upside, but remember that it is important to protect your downside first. Selling before the top helps you protect your downside while allowing you to lock in profits.

## Achieve Superior Returns with Less Exposure

When thinking about what kind of returns they want from their investments, most people talk about return on equity (ROE), which is the amount of money that is returned to an investor based on his ownership in a stock. I believe that there is a more important metric: return on investment. ROI measures the efficiency of one's investments. It is a metric that professional traders, hedge funds, and private equity firms use to measure performance when reporting to their own investors. ROI, which is a much more sophisticated measure than ROE, means getting the best possible return with the least amount of risk.

We know that there are 365 days in the year. Let's assume your goal is to make 10 percent on your investments in the coming year. My goal—and what so much of this book is about—is to make you a more efficient investor, meaning that I will help you either to make 10 percent in a shorter time frame in which you are taking on less risk, or to get a greater return, say 15 percent, in that same period of time. That is what it means to achieve a greater return on your investment.

How do you achieve that? By adhering to all of the investing tenets I have provided thus far. Entrances and exits are a large part of increasing your ROI. You have to be ready to change and adapt whenever the situation calls for it. By getting in—and out—of the market at the optimal times, you will increase your returns and lower your risk. By being underweight and overweight in the right sectors at the right times, by making appointments with the market, by using trailing stops, and by consistently evaluating the securities in your portfolio, you will almost assuredly increase the return on your investment and reach your financial goals faster than other investors who are less prepared to make the necessary adjustments at the right times.

We've covered a lot of ground so far. By now, I hope you are no longer thinking of a potential investment simply as a good company at a good price. Value investing, buy-and-hold investing, or whatever you want to call that old paradigm, is no longer enough to lock in profits over the long haul. Instead, you should understand by now that each investment must be researched, planned, calculated, and controlled. You should know before you make a trade at what price you'll buy—and at what price you'll sell. You need to know what volume tells you about the momentum of a stock. You also need to know that putting in place protective measures like stop loss orders will help you limit your downside and maximize your winners. Put all of those skills together, and you'll soon be executing like a pro while you buy high and sell higher.

But there are more lessons to be learned. In the next chapter, we'll talk more about what it means to be at market weight, underweight, and overweight.

# Maintain Position Flexibility

A concept that you'll hear professional investors bandy about a lot is "position flexibility." What it essentially means is keeping a war chest of cash at the ready for those moments when an opportunity that you have been waiting for finally appears. There are a number of techniques, such as adjusting the weights on the individual investments in your portfolio, that fall under the rubric of position flexibility. In this chapter, I'll walk you through some of these key techniques that will prevent you from getting handcuffed when markets turn volatile and will improve your all-around agility as an investor. You'll also learn why "3" is a magic number.

So what does position flexibility really mean? It means leaving yourself in a position to take advantage of the very few market anomalies that present themselves every year as investing opportunities. What does that mean? Let's say that you have $100,000 to invest. You've created your annual investment strategy, done your homework, and kept your investing appointments in order to build your portfolio. You're diversified across assets and sectors. Depending on factors such as your age, risk tolerance level, income expectations, and so forth, let's say for the sake of simplicity and purely as an illustration that you've decided to allocate your portfolio as $75,000 to stocks and $25,000 to other assets.

During the year, you monitor your investments regularly in order to determine whether it's time to sell positions (that is, move to an underweight position) or to add to positions (move to an overweight position). But you also need to keep an eye on any new investing opportunities that may arise (as long as those new opportunities fit within the parameters of your investing strategy). That means that at least a portion of your portfolio has to be liquid enough for you to pounce when those opportunities arise. And that means that part of that "other assets" category needs to be in cash or other highly liquid assets.

Position flexibility is crucial to "buy high, sell higher" investing. In this chapter, we'll take a closer look at this important aspect, including weighting the holdings in your portfolio.

## Overweight, Market Weight, Underweight

Throughout this book, we've talked about the importance of devising your investing strategy before you actually put any money into an asset. Part of your strategy means you need to leave yourself enough room—in the form of liquidity—to invest in those rare opportunities that may fit your strategic investing goals but aren't necessarily part of your original plan. Position flexibility does not mean waiting for something—anything—to pop up arbitrarily and reveal itself as a solid investment opportunity. Instead, it requires you to have some expectations about sectors or securities in which to invest when the technical and fundamental indicators are right. So, when I talk about position flexibility, I am talking about having the flexibility to be able to invest in things that might be unknown to you when you devise your strategy, though not in assets that are alien to you or do not fall within your overall knowledge base.

For example, let's say that in May 2010, the BP oil spill catastrophe in the Gulf of Mexico focused your attention on the energy sector and what its potential might be for the remainder of the year. You determined that based on your overall investing strategy and the fundamentals and technicals of the market, the timing might be right to invest in this sector. Had you maintained position flexibility, you would have been able to invest in an opportunity that was showing signs of confidence.

Although much of the overall market had been struggling, the energy market was showing signs of opportunity, primarily in May and June (though there wasn't necessarily a clear cause-and-effect relationship between the struggling market and the BP oil spill). Between April and August 2010, the price of oil averaged about $77. Before the BP oil spill, the price of oil was above $80. After the spill, the market sold off through the summer. For example, the Oil Services Holders ETF (OIH), which we will discuss in more depth in chapter 8, dropped to $89.48 on June 1, the lowest level it had traded at since July 13, 2009 (see figure 7.1).

On June 8, OIH traded at $89.63. That day, it failed to break the June 1 low, and it rallied all the way up to $92.64. That was

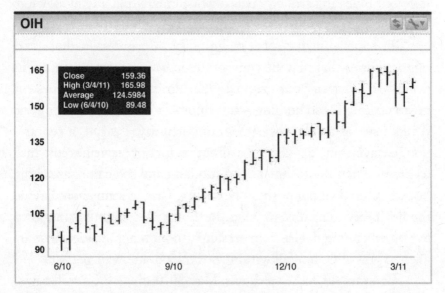

Figure 7.1: OIH Price Chart, June 2010–March 2011

a tremendous opportunity. It was a chance to buy OIH as it was moving higher and showing signs of confidence: by early June, OIH was doing great relative to the S&P 500; by December 2010, OIH was trading above $135, and by May 2011, it was at $160. An expectation of confidence and position flexibility would have put you in great shape to go market weight or even overweight to make the most of a golden opportunity.

### Increments of Three

So how do you determine how much capital to dedicate to particular investments and how much to keep aside for opportunities that may arise? This is the crux of maintaining position flexibility. When we think about maintaining position flexibility, we want to think in increments of three, and by that we're referring to weightings: overweight, market weight, or underweight. So 3 = overweight, 2 = market weight, and 1 = underweight. For instance, let's say your maximum allocation to any given stock is $18,000. That means that at $18,000, you would be overweight. At $12,000, you would be market weight, and at $6,000, you would be underweight.

You can think of weightings in terms of both dollars and shares. Essentially, it's the same thing, and one way of thinking is really no better or worse than the other. So you can think of overweight, market weight, and underweight in terms of dollars, shares, or even a percentage of your portfolio.

For example, Nike (NKE) had been an overweight position for me until the first quarter of 2011. I'm a believer in the Nike story for a number of reasons. For starters, affluent consumers have been a major contributor to Nike's success. In addition, only 37 percent of Nike's revenue comes from North America. Another 27 percent comes from Europe, the Middle East, and Africa. It gets another 14 percent from Asia and the Pacific and 11 percent from emerging markets. A cheap dollar really benefits Nike. Affluent consumers plus cheap dollars equals good things for Nike, which is one of those companies that fits the thesis of the decade of the Emerging Market Consumer, which we talked about earlier.

In 2010, Nike showed classic signs of acceleration in terms of volume (see figure 7.2). *Volume* is a measure of shares traded. An *acceleration of volume* refers to the rate at which the number of shares traded changes. (We'll discuss volume more in the next chapter when we talk about recognizing momentum changes.)

In September 2010, I went overweight in Nike as it hit reference points in the 50-day and 100-day moving averages. At the time, it was trading in the mid-$70s. By December 2010, Nike got as high as $92.49. But then a poor earnings report meant that Nike likely was going to slide lower.

As a result, I needed to scale back from an overweight position to a market weight position. And I had no problem doing that. Why? Because I was able to lock in a little bit of profit that I had in Nike and because, looking back, I hoped that someone would tell me I made a mistake selling some of my shares. That might

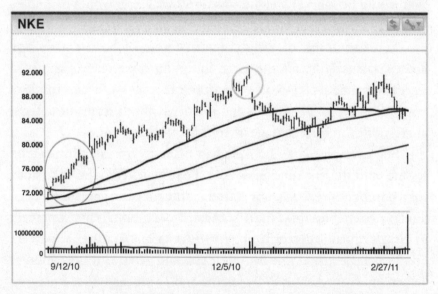

Figure 7.2: Nike (NKE) Volume & Price Chart, September 2010–March 2011

sound strange, but the fact is that I still was a believer in the stock. I still had confidence in it. I didn't sell my entire position. Instead, I took some profits and sold only part of my position—moving from overweight to market weight—thereby maintaining position flexibility for when the stock moves higher.

I liked Nike. I didn't really want to sell half, but, in reality, that was the right thing to do. In December 2010, after that bad earnings report, I got out of half of my Nike position. But I was still long Nike at overweight throughout the fall on the remaining half of my position. In March 2011, though, there was another horrible earnings report. So, I sold the other half. This was a case of being on the right side of discipline. I did my research, and it told me it was time to get out. How much I liked Nike didn't matter. The data said it was time to move out of an overweight position.

When we talk about weightings, we're looking at two things: a market benchmark (like the S&P 500) and your own portfolio. You always want your overall portfolio to beat the benchmark—otherwise you might as well just be investing in an index fund. Your portfolio as a whole needs to outperform the benchmark. You can tell whether you're beating it in an overweight position by determining whether it is, in fact, beating the S&P 500 (or whatever market index you're using) and asking whether a particular holding is an all-star in your portfolio. You want the biggest holdings in your portfolio to be the best performers. Your overweight holdings should be the all-stars, and the all-stars on your team should command the biggest percentages of your salary cap.

Institutional investors do this all the time. We talked earlier in the book about "window dressing," which is when institutional investors want to show their holdings in the best light when earnings reports are due. Individual investors can do the same thing. To do this, you need to track the data in quarterly statements. You might create a chart of your own; you might keep notes. But whatever you do, you need to read the quarterly statements and reports so that you can track performance and make sure your positions are at the correct weightings.

Let's take a closer look at weightings. In an overweight scenario, you want all hands on deck. You are, in essence, saying that this particular asset is going to account for a large chunk of your portfolio. When you go overweight on a particular investment, you're basically identifying that investment as the superstar that is going to account for a big chunk of your return for the year.

In a market weight scenario, you're essentially saying that you expect this holding to keep pace with the market. That's all you expect it to do. At market weight, you're just biding time. You're ready to spring into action. You believe the story, waiting for the right moment to move. That's not to say that being at market weight is a waste of time. Rather, keeping an asset at market weight allows you the time and space to monitor the market for changes (such as remarkable earnings reports or shifts in price and/or volume) that may precipitate a move to overweight or underweight. Being at market weight keeps you poised to move back to overweight when confidence returns.

When you're underweight, you're clearly playing defense. In an underweight environment, you believe that the confidence story is weak at best. You may believe that other investors have wrongly taken an overweight position and that they are going to crash and burn or make other sizable mistakes. You may believe that momentum may be poised for change. Out of that comes opportunity, and you'll be ready to adjust your weighting because you have enough liquidity to maintain the kind of position flexibility that allows you to do so.

So how do you determine weightings? Using your analysis—fundamental and/or technical—of the asset, you create a strength index for an individual asset based on your understanding of the asset, your confidence in it, and your conviction about the asset. Couple that with your research of how you expect that asset to perform based on the broader market and the broader asset class to determine the weighting you should give that individual asset.

A strength index can be customized to suit your needs and goals. You might create a strength index based on a simple 1–10 scale, where 10 is the best. Let's then say that you determine that the strength of the overall market is at a 9. Your research has lent you confidence in the security you've been looking at. With a strength index rating of 9 and the confidence you have in the asset, you should have the conviction to go overweight. If you feel that the strength of the overall market is dipping toward, say, a 6, you should challenge yourself and strongly consider moving to market weight or even underweight. Your strength index should help you determine the weighting of individual holdings in your portfolio. It can serve as a red flag—a buy sign or a sell sign—to help you determine whether you need to add to (or subtract from) a position.

In March 2009, when the entire world embraced pessimism, how many people out there truly had the capital to step into the marketplace and take advantage of unique buying opportunities, whether it be to the corporate bond market or to equities themselves, whatever their allocation was? How many investors had within their portfolio the ability in March 2009 to play offense and acquire assets? Very few. Rather, most people were reeling and thrown back on their heels after the crash in the fall of 2008. Most did not have position flexibility. But investors who had maintained position flexibility would have been in great shape to take advantage of the market. So let's take a look at what happened that made March 2009 a good entrance point for investors.

Back in 2002, the S&P 500 hit a multi-year low of 768. That low set a new floor for the S&P 500, a floor that we didn't see again until November 2008, in the midst of the liquidity crisis (see figure 7.3). On November 21, 2008, the S&P 500 hit a low of 741, breaking through a support level that had been in place for six years. By breaking through that point, the market set yet a new floor, indicating that investors had lowered their expectations and that the market could go even lower.

By January 6, 2009, the market rallied to 943. That was a

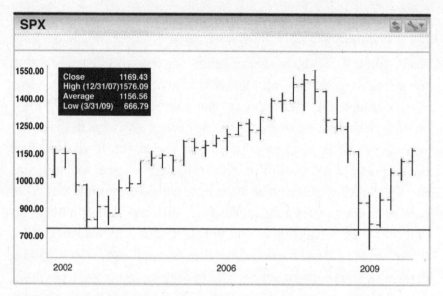

Figure 7.3: S&P 500, December 31, 2001–March 31, 2010

big bump, a nice run-up. Some investors could have played that, setting a stop-out point in the high 700s. I didn't make that play, however, because it was the end of the year, a time when I always like to be light in my positions (market weight or underweight). At the beginning of the year, I like to keep a wait-and-see attitude. (Remember my advice against trading at the end of the year and at the beginning of quarters.)

That wait-and-see attitude paid off as the S&P 500 slid down to 666 by March 6, 2009. The technical and fundamental analysis I performed indicated to me that I should step back and stay out, and so I did. My analysis told me that this was the kind of "black swan" event where I knew that the fundamentals and the technicals, both in the short term and over the next six to nine months, would show only limited opportunity for improvement. (Popularized by Nassim Nicholas Taleb in his 2007 book, black swan events are surprising, impactful events that in retrospect can be rationalized or explained.) I asked myself, *Is there more pain to come?* I thought there was. I recognized that Main Street America was still left holding some pretty bad positions in the market and that further liquidation would come. I wasn't pessimistic so much as I was anticipating or expecting that more waves of selling would come. My experience told me that this wasn't just a tremor.

In November, when the market declined, a lot of people had thought that was the end of it, that the sell-off was over. That the capitulation moment had passed. But I didn't believe it. I didn't think most people realized the severity of the crisis. That's where my wait-and-see-attitude paid off. Though I could have made some money between November and January, I remembered one of the first rules of investing: protect the downside. Had I been in the market between January and March, I would have lost any gains from the preceding three months.

Though technically the market was trending down in March, fundamentally there were some signs of confidence. A few fundamentals put me on watch: the bond markets, some of the bigger technology names within the NASDAQ, and some signs coming from China. In the bond markets, credit spreads began to tighten in March 2009 after having widened since September 2008. In the NASDAQ, some of the biggest names were holding their own. (The *credit spread* is the difference between Treasury securities and non-Treasury securities like corporate bonds. The tightening meant that investors felt certain key American corporations were creditworthy again.) For instance, even as the market was making new lows in March 2009, Apple was stabilizing. It never broke below its January 2009 low (see figure 7.4).

In addition to Apple, IBM was showing signs of confidence. On November 21, 2008, IBM traded at a low of $69.50. It never got near that again. From March 6 to March 9, 2009, while the rest of the market was trading lower, IBM was rallying toward $85 (see figure 7.5). Apple and IBM were showing signs of confidence, telling me that we were beginning to see the end of the "capitulation moment" (that's when markets plummet because so many investors

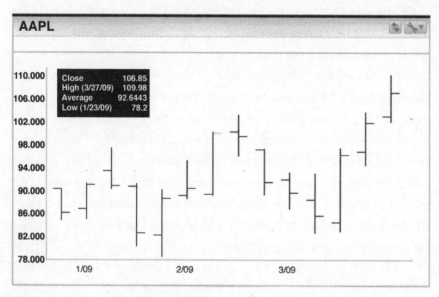

Figure 7.4: Apple Weekly Chart, January–March 2009

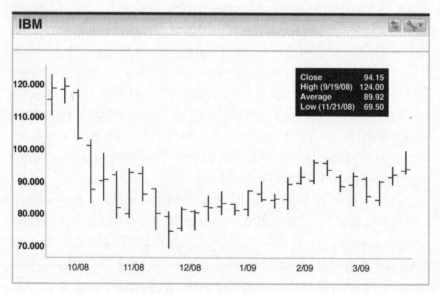

Figure 7.5: IBM Weekly Chart, September 19, 2008–March 27, 2009

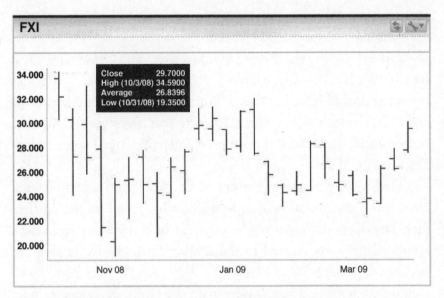

Figure 7.6: FXI Weekly Chart, October 2008–March 2009

are so disgusted with the market that they throw in the towel and sell off much of their portfolios).

Some signs from China also were giving me confidence. On October 26, 2008, the iShares China 25 Index Fund (FXI) traded at a low of $19.35. That was the ultimate low. While the market was still melting down, FXI had already recovered to $24 (see figure 7.6).

Some fundamentals were pointing toward growing confidence, but technically the market wasn't giving me a point of reference. The November low for the S&P 500—741—had created a new floor, but now with the market at 666, that low of 741 became a new ceiling. I knew we had to bust through that ceiling before it would be time to move to an overweight position. That would prove that there was momentum and confidence.

Sure enough, within a week, the market broke through 741, giving me a new reference point and telling me it was time to get back in the market. So, right away, I was back in. I had maintained the position flexibility to allow me to make the most of this opportunity.

On March 12, the S&P 500 closed at 750. On March 13, it was at 756. By Tuesday, March 17, it closed at 778. At that point, investors should have been back in the market. The fundamentals and the technicals were there to indicate that investors should have been in. But what kind of position should they have taken? How heavily should they have gotten in?

Here's the thing: the run-up in the S&P 500 during March 2009 was a classic example of how "buy high, sell higher" differs from buy-and-hold investing. A buy-and-hold investor would have remained fully committed to the market throughout the free-fall between October 2008 and March 2009. His capital—his liquidity—would have been tied up in assets that were tanking, leaving him no room to buy confidence when the market came back. So, the extent to which an investor should have gotten back into the market would have depended on his position flexibility. If he was just sitting back while the market rallied in March 2009, hoping to get back to even, chances are he wasn't liquid enough and that he hadn't maintained position flexibility. If you ever have reason to doubt the importance of position flexibility, just consider how frustrating that scenario was: you spot a rally and yet you have no cash to put into the market; instead, you have a zombie portfolio.

Institutional investors knew in March 2009 that it was time to be back in the market. They could go from completely under-weight to completely overweight because they had maintained position flexibility and were liquid enough to get back into the market when the indicators were there. In contrast, most retail investors missed the rally. Too much of their capital was tied up in losing positions—positions that they were hoping would return to even. Without position flexibility, they were unable to jump in when the market rallied and so couldn't take advantage of a great investing opportunity.

The lesson is that position flexibility is as critical for individual investors as it is for institutional investors. Investors must maintain enough liquidity in their portfolios to make the most of opportunities. To quantify it, I would suggest that most investors—long-term investors—in a portfolio leave somewhere between 12 and 18 percent of their total capital in highly liquid investments so that in a moment of opportunity—some might call it an historic opportunity or even a generational opportunity—you're able to quickly transition those investments into dollars necessary to acquire distressed assets, or assets that at the time are viewed as distressed.

*Distressed assets* are those securities of companies that may be viewed as unprofitable or otherwise in dire financial straits. Often, the prices of these otherwise worthy investments are depressed, and they may, in fact, be undervalued. They can be risky, but they also may be poised for quick profits—meaning they often can be investing opportunities. The trick is to buy confidence by doing your homework in order to make sure that you're buying assets with upside potential. Otherwise, you're just buying low in hopes of selling higher, which, as we've mentioned before, is like catching falling knives.

Recognizing opportunities when they arise can be a challenge for investors. It requires you to do your research and keep your eyes on those securities that might be poised to move in your favor. One question investors might ask is "How big of an opportunity am I looking for?" The answer depends in part on your own investing goals and strategy, but even a few cents can make a difference.

In fact, sometimes the smartest investments come in small increments. Citigroup offers a good example of this. In late 2010, Citigroup(C) was trading at a discount relative to its banking peers. As a result, the stock saw a price gap in late December (see figure 7.7).

In December 2010, the U.S. Treasury divested itself of Citigroup (except for the warrants, which had a nominal effect on the stock). That led to a two-cent price gap higher from $4.50 to $4.52. Even that two-cent difference was an opportunity for

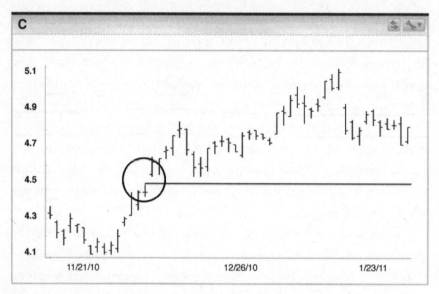

Figure 7.7: Citigroup Price Chart, November 2010–January 2011

investors. Although some professionals may have believed that a two-cent price gap was too tight, I felt it was time for investors to increase their holdings—to move to market weight or even over-weight. The fact that the Treasury had divested itself of Citigroup was a positive sign for investors, making Citigroup a good opportunity. For investors who already were holding Citigroup the time was right for them to buy more because the potential was there for the stock to move toward $5.00. One sign of that potential came in January 2011, when Citigroup announced earnings of $10.6 billion for 2010, its first full-year profit since the liquidity crisis of 2008–09. It's moments like this when investors really want to take advantage of maximizing a winning position. Why? Because the stock was showing signs of confidence.

Let's take a closer look at some of those signs. At the end of April 2010, Citigroup fell below $4.50. It didn't trade above that level again until November 5. On that day, and again on November 8, the stock opened at $4.52 (see figure 7.8).

After that, though, Citigroup struggled, falling back to $4.11.

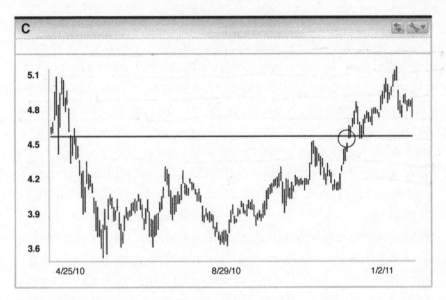

Figure 7.8: Citigroup, April 2010–January 2011

But on December 6, it finally climbed back up toward $4.50. What was once a resistance level became a support level. The next day, after the Treasury announced that it would divest itself of Citigroup, the low hit $4.54. So we had a price gap between $4.50 and $4.54. What this told us is that there was a little acceleration to the upside. At that point, investors could have put a stop loss order in place at $4.50. Some people may view that as a tight stop, but for a stock like Citigroup trading at under $5 per share, it isn't.

With just a four-cent window, a trade like this may be difficult to make for a lot of investors, but it's one you have to make if you want to take advantage of opportunities. You have to have the discipline to get to your position and put your stop in above $4.50. When I set that stop for myself, I got a lot of feedback from people who asked why I would get out below $4.50. But here's the thing: I'm not getting out below $4.50 for all of Citigroup—only for a portion of my holdings.

Let me explain further. Let's say you owned 300 shares of Citigroup. My suggestion would be that you buy 200 more shares. Put a stop in on those 200 new shares that you just bought. Remember, you are still long 300 shares as a core holding, so now you're holding 500 shares. My advice is to put a stop on the new portion of your overall holding, so, in this instance, a stop on the new 200 shares. Then, just forget about the other 300 shares. Just leave them alone. By putting a stop on a portion of a holding, it allows investors to take advantage of an opportunity and protect the downside at the same time. If the stock does fall, your stop is in place, helping to minimize any losses. But if the stock keeps going up, your position flexibility allows you to increase your overall holdings and maximize a winner. (Remember, too, that you can always use trailing stops when signs indicate that confidence is growing, as we discussed in chapter 6.) The good news on Citigroup is that it topped $5 in January 2011. (My thesis was correct: Citigroup reached $5 before it ever dipped to $4.50.)

Being able to add to a position—to move to an overweight position from a market weight position, or to a market weight position from an underweight position—likely will require you to dip into your cash reserves. Some people have asked me about how much cash an investor should keep on hand when they are overweight, market weight, or underweight. I am a firm believer that investors should keep some cash on hand even when overweight. How much? When overweight, you can still keep 5 to 15 percent in cash. You should keep 15 to 25 percent in cash when at market weight, and between 25 and 50 percent in cash when underweight. However, when you are underweight, you could have as much as 70 percent in cash.

Just remember that it's okay to be in cash. In fact, it's important to set aside some cash as a rainy day fund. And having a sunny day fund isn't a bad idea, either.

### Rainy Days and Sunny Days

Most people think of setting aside cash for rainy days—those emergencies that require immediate action and some liquidity to allow you to handle them. But cash also should be set aside for sunny days—those opportunities that may prove to be investing diamonds in the rough. Everyone should have a rainy day fund (most experts recommend keeping at least six months' worth of living expenses in an emergency fund separate from your investing capital), but you also should consider a sunny day fund. A sunny day fund is for the moment when the market's coming off the bottom. It's for the moment when everyone's chasing to get in, and it gives you the flexibility to get ahead of the herd.

Whichever you choose, or whatever you call it, these funds should be in cash. If not in cash, they should at least be in highly liquid assets. They should be assets that you could turn into tradable capital within twenty-four hours, such as money market accounts or even some blue-chip stocks such as Coca-Cola (KO), HJ Heinz (HNZ), and Walmart (WMT). The key is to move with the market: play defense when the market is pulling back. In that situation, you are in preservation-of-capital mode. This way you will have the cash on hand when things turn around or a great opportunity comes along and you're ready to pull the trigger. Keeping some cash on hand will ensure that you have the position flexibility you need when the market signals you to become more aggressive by increasing your holdings or adding to existing positions.

These percentages are unscientific and as such should not be considered as hard-and-fast rules, but more like general guidelines based on how I invest my own portfolio. The key is that even when you have a significant amount of cash, the money that you do have in the market has to be in those high-confidence names like Salesforce.com (ticker: CRM) or F5 Networks (FFIV) or Riverbed (RVBD)—that is, the real growth stories of the year (those were some of the names to have in 2010). That's what institutional investors do: they make sure that their capital is in the high fliers that are likely to deliver returns of 30 or 40 percent when the overall market is up only 10 percent. That's one of the differences between investing and owning a professional sports franchise. Only one team can own A-Rod or LeBron, but any and all investors can own shares of CRM or FFIV.

Some investors may question whether they can have too much set aside in cash. The answer is no. But the real questions are "How much cash do I need to protect myself from the downside?" and "How much cash do I need on hand in order to take advantage of investing opportunities?" There are no absolute answers, but you should never be afraid to go into cash so you can take advantage of those rare investing opportunities.

## Analyze Your Worst-Case Scenario

Position flexibility leaves you the room to move when market opportunities call for it. But how do you gauge whether your portfolio has enough flexibility? One way is to analyze the worst-case scenario for each holding in your portfolio and determine what would happen if everything tanked at once.

Part of doing your homework means conducting risk analysis. This is something you should be doing constantly. With that, you should be looking at your entire portfolio and asking yourself what kind of hit you would take if everything in it went the wrong way. Analyzing your worst-case scenario reveals how much position flexibility you really have. Most investors don't perform risk analysis on their own portfolios, but it is something that every investor should do.

What would happen, for instance, if an up market turned around and the S&P 500 sank by, say, 20 percent in two months? How much of a loss could you withstand on your entire portfolio, assuming that you did not get out of any of your positions along the way? Not only does risk analysis help determine whether your individual holdings are weighted properly, it also can help you determine if you're over- or underweighted in particular sectors. Position flexibility isn't just about dollars and shares, it's also about sectors: you want to make sure your holdings are correctly weighted across different sectors in order to have a diversified portfolio.

For instance, let's say your portfolio holdings come from nine different sectors. Let's also say you're overweight in three of those sectors. That comes at the expense of your other holdings. Why? If you have a finite amount of money to invest, you can't be overweight in every sector or in every holding. You have to, then, be at market weight or underweight in other sectors and holdings within your portfolio. That doesn't mean, though, that you're not diversified. As long as your holdings reach across those nine sectors, regardless of whether you're overweight, market weight, or underweight, your portfolio should still be well diversified.

How do you know, though, if you're overallocated to a particular sector? If you're overweight in a particular holding? Analyze your worst-case scenario, and if it reveals that you are over- or underweight in too many holdings or in too many sectors, chances are you are also over- or underallocated in those areas and that your portfolio is not as diversified as it should be.

Let's look at another example. Let's say your portfolio is 100 percent in equities. What happens when the stock market goes into free fall? Are you willing to sell some of your holdings to raise cash? Which of the stocks that is falling do you move to market weight or underweight? What happens to most investors is that they do nothing. What's their motivation to sell equities and raise cash? Far less than it is when the market is not in free fall. In a free-falling market, investors have to take a loss on everything, and it goes against human nature to admit complete and utter defeat. So investors remain frozen, often in denial, and more often than not do nothing.

You always want to be able to weather a storm. So never put yourself in a position where you're forced to take a loss, where you're not liquid, where you're overallocated in an asset class or a sector. There always has to be some sort of balance.

Before we leave the topic of position flexibility and how to weight your investments, it is important to note that there will be moments when being flexible will come into conflict with your investing plan. This is one of those instances where you realize that if investing were merely painting by numbers, everyone would be George Soros. After reading this chapter, you undoubtedly now understand that the way to avoid becoming overallocated in a market, whether it's up or down, is to not increase the value of an asset that's moving against you. This challenges the notion of dollar cost averaging, which we discussed in chapter 6. Dollar cost averaging is a great tool for planning, but savvy investors are able to recognize when to set tools aside in favor of common sense.

For example, when the markets are slipping and investors are quitting, I advise investors to step back. I suggest that investors sit on their hands during capitulation moments. Resist the temptation to join the herd and sell into the panic. If you see one of these moments, it is better to step back and do nothing—even for your overweight positions. Just watch everyone give up, and maintain your capital and position flexibility. If, for example, the capitulation moment occurs on a Monday, it is better to sit back and wait and see what the reaction is on Tuesday and Wednesday as well. The first time I would advise an investor to enter the market with new money in the midst of one of these moments would be late Wednesday or, better yet, Thursday.

## Flexibility Is Also in Your Mind

Sitting out during capitulation moments and other times when the market is acting erratically can be a challenge for investors. But taking a breather of this kind can help you maintain position flexibility in terms of your overall portfolio, and it also allows you to retain mental dexterity.

Good traders adapt to changing markets. And the fact is that the markets are always changing, whether they're changing from open outcry to electronic, whether from an equities-driven market to a fixed-income-driven market. In 2008–09, a lot of investors failed to understand the importance of corporate bonds in their portfolios. They didn't understand that when the recovery occurred in the capital markets, it was going to occur first in the corporate bonds market. Why didn't they understand? Because they weren't looking there. Instead, investors were thinking about equities and looking for a recovery there first—and they missed out as companies were getting their houses in order.

Let's take a closer look at that. The thing is that most recessions are different from one another, not just in scope, but also in the nature of the recession. The recession in Japan in the early 1990s was a corporate balance sheet recession. So was the 2001 recession in the United States. But the recession of 2008–09 was a consumer balance sheet recession. Because of that, corporations were in a much better position than consumers to recover more quickly. As a result, the health of corporations became a leading indicator of recovery because their debt burdens weren't as large and because they had more cash on hand. Corporate balance sheets were stronger than consumer balance sheets. Investors should have asked themselves whether it made more sense to invest in an equities market that was highly exposed to consumer spending or to invest in the bonds of corporations, which had better balance sheets.

Had you been locked in to an equities-only mind-set, you would have missed a great opportunity. So position flexibility is important, but mental flexibility is, too. Not only should you have your rainy day and sunny day funds in place and be ready to capitalize on those rare investing opportunities, but you also should be emotionally and mentally ready to move into those positions.

So how often should you be adjusting your portfolio to stay nimble and to be ready? For most investors, I'd suggest they adjust weightings perhaps six to eight times a year. What you don't want to do is day-trade or trade compulsively, both of which are fool's errands. Look at the market every day. But don't trade every day. Compulsive behavior is not a pathway to financial freedom.

Maturity is the antidote to compulsive investing. Maturity allows you to remain calm, to be in a better mental state to take advantage of investing opportunities, to read the markets better. It helps you weather capitulation moments. It can help you recognize more easily whether you are over- or underallocated in the markets in general or in a particular position.

For instance, if you're losing sleep, if you're worried about what's happening in the market, then you're likely overexposed. When I wake up every day, do I check in to see where the markets are? Sure I do. It's what I do for a living. I keep my eye on things. But I'm not having 2:00 a.m. stress. I'm not waking up in a sweat in the middle of the night. I'm not spending the entire night managing a position.

While you shouldn't be trading compulsively, you also should not be a slave to your original investing strategy. By all means, you want to stick to your plan, and you should rely on your team to help you do so. But you also need to remain flexible enough to be able to move when opportunities arise.

Institutional investors—professional traders—know that the key is to be tactical in executing their investing strategies. They're not trading every day or even every other day. Maybe they're making two trades a month. But they're being tactical about it. They're making trades that make sense within their individual investment strategies. They're playing offense instead of defense, and that allows them to strike first—to buy high and sell higher. Maintaining position flexibility allows you to be tactical, to invest offensively instead of defensively.

Maintaining mental flexibility, relying on your growing wisdom and maturity as an investor, will help you maintain position flexibility during times of change. And the fact is that the markets are constantly changing. You have to be ready to take advantage of changes and opportunities when they arise.

# 8

# Recognize Momentum Changes

Institutional investors typically get out of the market more quickly than retail investors. They act on information faster, and they are less emotional than the retail investor. They recognize momentum changes much sooner than most retail investors. In fact, I am constantly looking at the markets, the securities I own, and the macro environment to figure out if the story has changed for any of the assets I am holding. The key question I ask myself is this: has the reason for owning any of these securities changed?

Institutional investors like MBF ask this question all the time, and individual investors should ask it about their holdings, too. In the 1990s at MBF, we traded natural gas, oil, and oil-related commodities. However, in 1999, the year after the Asian crisis and the fall of Long Term Capital Management, the market for natural gas dried up. The Asian crisis, which actually started in Thailand in the summer of 1997, created fears that the financial debacle in Asia would spread to the rest of the world.

One of the by-products of that crisis was what happened to the price of commodities. How bad was it? In 1998, the price of natural gas traded between $1.61 and $2.71.* Remember that in late 2005 after Katrina, natural gas traded above $16 (in March 2011, natural gas was trading at around $4). There was no liquidity (meaning the volume was very low) and even less momentum. At MBF, we recognized the change in the commodity story early on, so we knew that we had to take drastic action. Asia's increased demand for resources during a period of fast economic growth in the early 1990s had led to an upswing in the commodities markets. But by the late 1990s, that same demand, among other things such as slowing exports and growing deficits, eventually led to economic crisis. This crisis, in turn, took the commodities market down with it. That's when we at MBF started to trade stocks instead of commodities.

We recognized that the investing landscape and the momentum had changed. We caught a good wave in the equities market in 1998 and 1999. In 1999, natural gas traded between $1.62 and $3.28, so it was still depressed. Oil was declining, too. In 1998, oil fell to $11 after the Asian crisis hit. By December 21, 1998, the price of oil hit $10.35. The momentum had changed: commodities had gone from a confidence market to a catch-the-falling-knives market. One of the primary reasons for the change in momentum was that the confidence game had shifted from commodities to equities. We had always been in the business of buying confidence, so we knew when it was time to cut our losses and maximize our winners, and there was no better confidence market in the late 1990s than the equities market.

In early 2000, we recognized that the story was about to change again. The dot-com crash was looming, and the signs were there: gushing news reports about high-flying IPOs built on little but hype and hope, chatter about yet another new paradigm, dot-com start-ups without business plans stealing top manage-

---

*In 1998, the price of oil traded between $10.35 and $18.06, which was one of the worst markets for oil I have ever seen.

ment from brick-and-mortar stalwarts. We had heard that kind of hype and noise before. We had seen it in the natural gas market in 1995, 1996, and 1997. During those three years, the price of natural gas surged in December but fell shortly after, taking back all our profits. On December 21, 1995, natural gas traded at $3.72. By January 10, 1996, it fell to $2.72. A similar thing happened the following year when natural gas hit $4.31 on December 18, 1996, falling to $1.88 by February 21, 1997. And the same thing the next year: natural gas hit $3.80 on December 27, 1997, and fell to $2.03 on January 29, 1998. We learned from our experience. As a result, when we saw that kind of shift again in 2000, we moved our proprietary traders out of equities back into commodities. That proved to be a very good move.

We did a great job of protecting our profits by focusing like a laser on risk management and by using tight trailing stop loss orders. We were so disciplined about using stop loss orders that our penchant for simultaneously placing buy and sell orders for commodities also worked beautifully for us when we traded equities. We weathered the dot-com crash of 2000–02 because of the tight stops we used (*tight stop* means placing the stop price not far below the share price). We knew at what price we would get into trades—and at what price we would get out. When the equities bubble popped, we were among the first ones out.

I don't tell these stories to brag about how great or how smart we were back then. The real takeaway is that the key to long-term success in any market depends on the investor's ability to recognize when the story has changed and the momentum has moved from one market to another, one sector to another, or one security to another. The best traders and investors I have ever seen had that ability— that all-so-rare quality to make a key move ahead of the pack, not behind it. The changes we made at MBF were macro changes from one market (commodities) to another (stocks). Chances are that the changes you will need to detect early involve micro decisions, such as when the momentum shifts from one stock to another.

One of the keys to recognizing momentum changes involves keeping track of your investments. The primary way I track my investments (and potential investments) is by keeping a notebook that details both the technical and fundamental stories of the stocks and other securities on my radar screen. Tracking individual investments is something that most retail investors simply don't do, which makes it more difficult to discern a genuine change in momentum.

But investors really should keep notes on each of their holdings. In fact, I have more than a dozen notebooks filled with data and information about investments I have held over the years, and I keep them all close at hand in my office (see figure 8.1). Not long ago I tried to keep these notes on my iPad, but I soon figured out that when I actually write something down, my retention is much better, so I went back to using the hard-copy notebooks. Through trial and error, you will find what way works best for you.

The key to making these notebooks a real help to you and your investment efforts is to play a game I like to call "Tell me something I don't know." That is essentially the game we play on the CNBC show *Fast Money*. When we invite an outside expert onto the show with us, we are really challenging him or her to tell us something that we don't know, whether it is a piece of data about a particular stock or something more macro-oriented involving the global economy.

In order to be a successful investor, you have to be a compulsive note taker. Your investment notebook should be packed with numbers and statistics, and because you're the manager of your own investments, you have to learn to know what those statistics mean.

For example, I like to know where each particular stock opened at the beginning of the most recent quarter. I also look at fundamentals, such as the company's earnings and the trajectory of its earnings, as well as at the volume and the trajectory of the volume of that stock as well. I also take a look at balance sheet strength

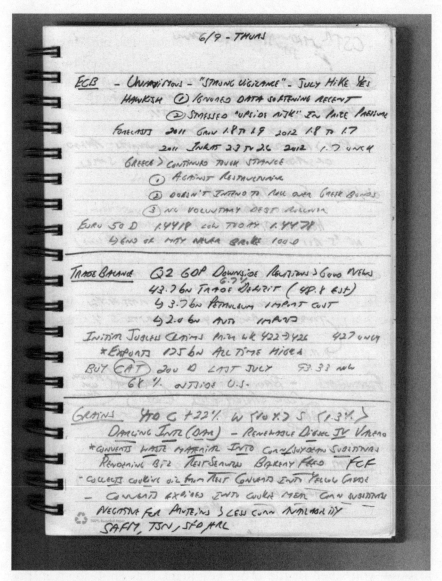

Figure 8.1: Sample of My Notebook

(how much money the company has in its coffers after paying off its debt), its dividend, etc. Since you are the primary decision maker when it comes to your own portfolio, you have to include the statistics and variables that are most important to you. You'll find that as you get to be more of an expert about the companies that you're following, you'll start uncovering one or two items that are not widely known—the home version of "Tell me something I don't know." I am not talking about inside information, but one or two items that may be overlooked by the majority of investors.

"Tell me something I don't know" is a game that is played in every institutional investment office conference room in America. I remember when I was at MBF, our owner, Mark Fisher, would hold regular meetings to see if he could learn one or two things that had the potential to alter his thinking about a security or the overall market. "Tell me something I don't know" was the reason Mark called these meetings. It would be Mark, me, and a dozen other people, talking about companies and the markets. To gain Mark's attention—and this is not unique to Mark; this happens at all Wall Street firms—traders would try to come up with new ideas that were not widely known. One person might talk about how the demand for oil was rising in China. Mark would abruptly say, "I know that. Next." People would throw out other ideas. "I know that. *I know that,*" Mark would shoot back. Everyone is that curt because time is so valuable on Wall Street. You want to capture the one or two things that everybody doesn't know. By keeping this notebook, you want to be able to play the same game with yourself and your own investing team.

### What's in My Notebook?

Let's take a look at a stock that I have owned throughout the years to show you some of the other key items that I jot down in my investment notebook. One stock that has been a favorite of mine is Freeport McMoRan Copper & Gold Inc. (FCX). While this is obviously a stock, it also serves as a proxy for copper (more so than gold, but gold as well). In order to trade this stock, I need to know what is going on with the price of copper. Is the price of copper rising? If so, this could be a good time to own FCX. I need to know about overall demand coming from developing countries. If growth numbers coming out of the BRIC countries like China are strong, then that might be another reason to own this stock. I also need to look at the company's most recent quarterly earnings. Are the earnings consistent with the growth stories coming out of the emerging markets? Is the trajectory of the earnings matching the fundamental story of strong demand for copper and oil? These are all things that should be jotted down in my investment notebooks.

Let's assume that I am getting conflicting information about the outlook for the stock. Let's assume that given the growth coming out of China, it seems that China can't buy enough copper (meaning copper demand from China is high). However, the most recent earnings report from Freeport shows less-than-stellar earnings that are down from the previous quarter. I keep those statistics in my notebook so I can check on these critical pieces of information like earnings growth (or lack of earnings growth). I like to know on a technical basis what the 52-week high is for the stock, as well as the 52-week low, the 50-day moving average, the 100-day moving average, and the 200-day moving average. I also  like to know the quarterly high in the stock price. I want to know where the stock opened in its most recent quarter. That's an important data point that a lot of individual investors overlook, because where a stock opens in its most recent quarter provides insight into institutional money flows within the quarter.

Assuming I kept good notes, I could look back and see that the stock began to gather strength during the third quarter of 2010. It started the quarter trading at about $60 per share, and within a month the stock hit $70 (a 16.67 percent increase). That means there had been positive flows of capital into the stock—an underlying strength that shows that there is positive sentiment about the copper and gold. These bits of intelligence are all in my notebook because I update it on a regular basis.

Of course, I probably update my notebook much more frequently than most retail investors because investing is what I do every day. You may find that updating your notebook once a quarter, once a month, or once a week works for you. Either way, it needs to include, at the bare minimum, information about price highs and lows, earnings, volume, and moving averages.

Investors also should include a few other key bits of information in their notebooks, including data about competitors. As a matter of course during all your research, you should be looking not only at the company you're targeting as a potential investment, but also at its primary competitor. For instance, let's say you're interested in the soft drinks market, and you believe that the market is poised for growth, so you're looking at Coke and Pepsi. You want to buy either one of those—but not both. Why? Because if you're wrong about the market and the market tanks, you want to limit your exposure. So, into your notebook goes information about both companies. You want to look at which of the two shows the most strength, which seems best positioned for growth. Track that information in your notebook, updating it with data from such sources as quarterly earnings statements, annual reports, and so forth.

Another important piece of information that also should be in your investing notebook: the name of the CEO (and perhaps a quick snapshot of his credentials). I am always surprised when investors can't name the CEOs of the companies they own. Once again, I mean no disrespect to investors, but it is almost comical when an investor can't name the CEO of a company that might be his key holding. That makes no sense to me! How can you not know who the CEO is? You have to know that, and that should be in your notebook along with any key management shifts at the top of the company. That's because different CEOs will be perceived to have certain strengths, and a change at the top of the firm can surely make a big difference in the stock price over time.

Here is a prime example of how a change at the top can make a big difference at a company. Mark Hurd was given the top job of CEO of Hewlett Packard (HP) in April 2005, taking the reins from CEO Carly Fiorina. Although he was a relative unknown, Hurd was a great fit for HP. He was known to be a solid operating manager, and he drove the stock price from about $20 per share to more than $50. Under Hurd's leadership, HP shot past IBM to become the world's largest technology company.

However, in August 2010, Hurd was ousted from the company amid charges of alleged sexual misconduct (and alleged inaccurate expense reports submitted to conceal the transgression). How did Wall Street react to the Hurd ouster? Not well. Before the announcement of his demise, the stock traded north of $46 per share. By the end of the month of his departure, HP traded below $38 per share, a fall of more than 17 percent in about twenty-five days, as shown in figure 8.2.

It also is worth noting that upon the announcement of Hurd's departure, daily volume surged to 200 million shares, compared to an average daily volume of about 2.5 million shares. That volume told investors that the departure of this CEO was a big deal and that Wall Street would likely continue to "punish" the company for some time to come. And it has: after struggling toward a high of $48.99 in February 2011, the stock traded back down at $43.10

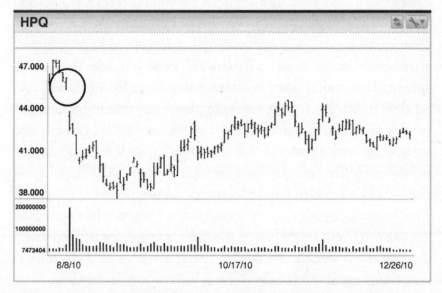

Figure 8.2: Hewlett-Packard Price and Volume Chart, July–December 2010

in March, well below the $50 range it had once reached. But other than Hurd's sudden departure, little had changed at HP. The fundamentals of the company basically remained the same. This example clearly shows is why it is important to know who the CEO is and how he or she is perceived by Wall Street.

## Volume and Momentum Are the Keys

As we have discussed throughout the book, volume can be a key indicator of a change in momentum of the market or of a particular security. In order to increase your investor's quotient, you need to understand why volume—of shares traded daily on an exchange and of a particular stock—is such an important metric. When volume declines, generally momentum in a given direction declines with it. When you buy a stock, you are looking for an appreciation in volume. Falling volume is the equivalent to a loss of momentum, so why would you want to invest then? That's a false opportunity.

I like to look at the slope or trajectory of things. For example, let's say you are heavily invested in a number of NASDAQ stocks. Check the 30-day moving average of the volume on NASDAQ and check out the slope (you can do this on Yahoo! Finance, Google Finance, or another financial website). An upward slope indicates increasing volume, while a downward slope indicates decreasing volume. If the total daily volume of shares traded on NASDAQ is below its 30-day moving average, then you want to be sure that you are not trading more actively than the volume suggests. If you are actively trading when volume is either going sideways (staying steady) or down, you may be a compulsive investor. And compulsive behavior tends to lead to losses, as we mentioned in chapter 7. The frequency of your trades should properly match the slope of the volume on whatever exchange you are trading most actively (e.g., the New York Stock Exchange [NYSE] or the NASDAQ). This is something you should be checking at least on a quarterly basis.

Volume also should be a key factor in determining the number of positions you are holding in your portfolio. If you begin to see volume decreasing across the board—in the NASDAQ, the NYSE, the Dow, and even in commodities—that is a sign that you should be reducing holdings and overall positions.

Let's use an example that I vividly recall to drive the point home. In February and early March 2009, volume on all the key stock market exchanges declined. When volume starts to wane, that's when you want to lighten up on your positions and own closer to nine positions than twenty-two. You do that because the light volume means that you do not have the wind at your back. You have no tailwind. I recognized this change and moved to an underweight position. By moving to underweight, I was freeing up investing capital for the moment when the market came back to life. That move allowed me to maximize winners and minimize losers.

So how would I know when it was time to get back in? How could I spot the momentum shift? I knew I had to keep an eye on the 30-day volume. Remember, when you begin to see the slope of the 30-day volume moving average begin to rise, that's when you want to acquire assets and add securities to your portfolio.

Volume is a factor not only over weeks and months and quarters; it also plays a role on a daily basis. The heaviest volume on any exchange occurs within the first hour and the last hour of the day. If you visit the trading floor of a big Wall Street firm, you will notice that the floor is far less populated in the middle of the day than it is at the end of the day (the best traders go for a long lunch at around 11:00 a.m. EST). That is one of the reasons volume drops during the day, and you never want to trade in that environment because momentum is falling with volume. By trading during those hours, all you are doing is taking on additional risk that is completely avoidable.

Let's assume that you do not heed this advice and buy a stock that is declining in volume. Then you need to check back thirty to sixty days later to check the price of that security and the volume. If the volume continues to decline, even if the price of the stock has gone up, cut back on your holdings. You may say, "Hey, that makes no sense. If the stock's going up, why should I cut back on my holdings?" The answer is simple: because there's no volume behind it to support the appreciation of the stock price. So that stock will eventually give up its gains and fall back to earth. There's nothing behind it that could support it.

Volume supports price action. One of the obstacles that existed in the stock market in the first half of 2010 was that the lack of volume failed to support the potential breakout that the equities market tried for in the first quarter. It was a classic example of the absence of volume leading to a frustrating market.

What is a "frustrating market"? I would define it as a market where the investor is extremely challenged to create any alpha at all. That doesn't mean the market flatlines. That means the market seems to find a certain center point and over a three- to six-month period of time vacillates north or south. But gravity always pulls it back to that center. That's a frustrating market.

However, volume should not be looked at in isolation. That's because there can be big volatility surges on down days, especially those days when the Dow falls by triple digits. I have seen instances where huge volume means the bottom in a stock—it's the liquidation or capitulation moment. That's why investors need to look at volume as well as price action to determine how fertile the trading environment is. However, more often than not, heavy volume means strong momentum, while the absence of volume indicates that investors should avoid the stock and/or the market as a whole.

## When an Earnings Surprise Means a Change in Momentum

When it comes to volume, several key events may signal a change is in the offing. For example, a company's earnings reports often can signal shifts in momentum, and it is up to the investor to do the research to figure out what is going on behind the scenes. Remember that earnings report release dates should be flagged on your investing calendar. Part of your homework should involve looking at where you can identify any earnings surprises.

Once again Yahoo! Finance is a great source of free information for retail investors. To learn of earnings surprises, go to Yahoo! Finance (www.finance.yahoo.com) and note the tabs across the top (even I was surprised at the amount of information available free on this site). Click on the tab "Investing" and go to "Stocks" on the drop-down menu, which will take you to what they call "Stock Research Center," which opens up a new menu. Then click on "Surprises" under the first section entitled "Company Earnings." Why are surprises such an important concept when it comes to sentiment and potential momentum changes?

Let's assume that you own Dell (DELL) stock, and for the most recent quarter the analysts' consensus is for quarterly earnings of 33 cents per share. However, when Dell reports earnings, it surprises to the upside with earnings of 45 cents, for a net surprise of 36 percent. Let's dig in to figure out what this surprise means.

Throughout the second half of 2010, Dell was an underperformer. It was challenged because institutional investors consider Dell part of the "old technology" story. Old technology stocks are the ones that performed well in the 1990s but stumbled badly in the 2000s amid the dot-com crash and for much of the rest of the decade. The sentiment surrounding Dell has been negative for quite some time. Other stocks that fall into this category include Microsoft, Intel, and Yahoo!

Once you learn of the Dell earnings surprise, you need to roll up your sleeves and do some investigative research. You have to figure out where the surprise came from. Is it due to a surge in demand for Dell products, which would be the most bullish reason for the earnings surge? Or was it because Dell cut back on expenses and jobs, so that the surprise was not due to increased demand, but because of better handling of the bottom line? Is this a one-time increase in earnings, or has something fundamentally changed within the earnings model, which allows them further earnings growth? Has the company unveiled a new product that is going to drive sales? This is a potentially classic story of "Tell me something I don't know" where you need to reevaluate the company's story.

That's part of the research process. There is the other side of this coin, and that also can be found at Yahoo! Finance. Return to the "Stock Research Center" and look at "Up/Downgrades" under the second item "Analyst Research." It is important to understand analysts' upgrades and downgrades and not to follow their advice blindly.

For example, let's say you learn that the investment company JP Morgan Chase (JPM) has been added to the Goldman Sachs Conviction Buy List with a price target that is 25 percent higher than the existing stock price. Even though I have more respect for Goldman's Buy List than any other financial firm's list, the one thing I don't want you to do is simply pull the trigger and buy the stock because Goldman Sachs says to. Instead, what you should do is note the upgrade in your investment notebook, including the date of the upgrade and the upside target price.

It is important to note here that I did not choose JP Morgan by chance. That happens to be a company that I often own. What has worked well for me after the stock has been upgraded is to watch that stock closely, seeing if it pulls back with any downdraft in the market. For instance, let's say that three weeks after the upgrade, the overall stock market falls by 3 to 4 percent and JP Morgan falls by 2 to 3 percent. The first thought I have is that this is a chance to buy a security that is surrounded by confidence, that has fallen in price for reasons not involving that company, and that has actually held up better than the overall stock market. JP Morgan is standing tall despite a headwind pushing the market back. Since I want to be in the confidence business, I see that as a buying opportunity in JP Morgan.

Going back to the Dell example, you want to look at the upgrade/downgrade list for that stock as well. A good analyst, or even a number of analysts, might have altered his opinion about that stock. If the earnings surprise did not prompt any analysts to alter their opinions about the stock, that tells you something important that also should be in your investment notebook. It may mean that the "surprise" wasn't much of a surprise after all, that the news already had been factored into the stock price, or, for instance, that analysts are waiting for more information before altering their opinions.

The other side of this equation involves a stock that is loved by everyone. Let's use a hypothetical example involving Apple (AAPL), since that's a stock that all retail investors and institutional investors seem to love. For purposes of this example, let's assume that Apple comes out with its earnings, and it is an earnings surprise to the downside. Let's assume that before the earnings release every analyst loves Apple. What do you do when the negative surprise is reported? Let's make a few more assumptions going into that surprise. Let's assume that every analyst has a "buy" recommendation on Apple and a price target that's much higher than the current price. Then we get this negative surprise in earnings. What's likely to happen is that most analysts will lower their price targets, and some may even downgrade the stock from a "buy" to a "hold." That's an immediate momentum change that the retail investor has to pick up on. You recall that earlier in the book I warned investors not to trade a stock immediately after a decision from the Federal Open Market Committee (FOMC), oil numbers, or unemployment numbers. But I did say that you can make a buy or sell decision based on an earnings report. This is an example of something that you can use to make an immediate decision. This is about a momentum change in the market and a fundamental change in the story of a stock.

I want you to get ahead of the analysts, which, in a situation like this, are almost assuredly going to downgrade the stock and lower the price target, and that's going to change the story of the stock. If you don't get out ahead of the analysts, you might be stuck with dead money for the next three to six months.

## Identifying Tomorrow's Confidence Stories

Finding tomorrow's confidence stories is something all investors should strive to do on a regular basis. That's the way to build alpha and find those rare companies that have the potential to break out and deliver the greatest returns. One of the biggest challenges in identifying these kinds of stocks is learning where to start. You might choose to start with earnings reports and see if you can learn something important there (a strong earnings surprise, as we discussed). Or perhaps a key technical indicator (say, a huge spike in volume) has changed for a given security.

For example, it could be something important like what we saw in the energy space in autumn 2010. That was when the 50-day moving average crossed above the 200-day moving average in the energy space for the first time since June 2009 (see figure 8.3). That very bullish technical indicator is important enough to warrant its own term: it is called the "Golden Cross." A Golden Cross occurs when a security's short-term moving average breaks above its long-term moving average. Any time you see a Golden Cross, you should pay particularly close attention to it and possibly begin to accumulate shares in that asset. The reason a Golden Cross does not signal an automatic buy is because you want to make sure that the fundamental story (e.g., earnings) matches the technical story. (In contrast to a Golden Cross is the "Death Cross." Considered a bearish indicator, a Death Cross occurs when a security's long-term moving average breaks above its short-term moving average. In this instance, you should consider selling shares in the asset.)

In the overall market, we saw a Golden Cross for the first time in four years in October 2010 when the Dow, S&P 500, and NASDAQ all achieved Golden Crosses (the Dow did it on the first of the month, and the S&P and NASDAQ did it about three weeks later). That move signaled what was about to happen in the stock market. The major averages achieved two-year highs as all

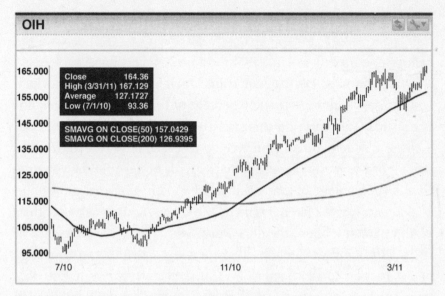

| OIH | | |
|---|---|---|
| Close | 164.36 | |
| High (3/31/11) | 167.129 | |
| Average | 127.1727 | |
| Low (7/1/10) | 93.36 | |

SMAVG ON CLOSE(50) 157.0429
SMAVG ON CLOSE(200) 126.9395

Figure 8.3: 2010 Chart of OIH with Golden Cross

three (the Dow, S&P, and NASDAQ) rallied to a point above the averages we saw just ahead of the Lehmann collapse in September 2008. From October 2010 to December 2010, the S&P rallied from 1,150 to 1,250.

A Golden Cross indicates that a bull market is looming, that confidence is growing. It's not necessarily an action signal. Rather, investors should consider a Golden Cross a sign to investigate whether the time is right to move to a market weight or overweight position. By no means an absolute indicator, a Golden Cross cannot precisely indicate when or for how long a rally might take place. But it can point to confidence stories, which is exactly what investors should be looking for.

## Follow the Institutions

One other key statistic I follow closely for every security that I consider buying is the percentage of a particular stock held by

institutions. Once again, I am looking to identify change. Not only do I want to look for the change, I also want to see how fast the change occurs.

For example, let's say I am thinking of buying a stock in which institutions hold more than 60 percent of the company's outstanding shares (you can find this statistic easily on most any financial website). When you do your weekly research on, say, each Thursday night when your spouse is out with his or her friends, you note that the percentage of that stock held by institutions has gone up to 70 percent. A week later, it is up to 72 percent, and a week after that, it is 74 percent. Then, the next week, you note a real difference in the institutional ownership. The company had reported earnings and surprised to the downside. You then perform your due diligence on the stock and note that three analysts have downgraded the stock. Two went from a "buy" to a "hold," and one went from an "outperform" to a "market neutral." Now the percentage of institutions that own that stock has fallen to 60 percent. When that happens, you want to do what the institutions are doing. Those institutions have looked at the stock with fresh eyes following the earnings report, and many have decided to sell their holdings. The fundamentals of that stock have changed, the story has changed, and the momentum has changed. When the story changes and the financial professionals change their view of a security, you need to change along with them and at least pare back on your holdings of that security to underweight.

Other changes in a company's story also could warrant paring back or selling your entire position in a stock. As discussed earlier, when a company has what is perceived to be a "superstar" leader, the price of that stock often has a premium built in based on the elite status of the company's CEO. Let's look once again at Mark Hurd and Hewlett-Packard.

On August 9, 2010, came the announcement that Hurd, considered by the Street to be a very effective leader, was leaving the company. Most institutions saw this as a real threat to the stock's price. That is because when Mark Hurd became CEO, he had very publicly announced that his number one priority was to grow earnings, and that he would pursue every avenue to do so. To achieve earnings growth, he would reduce the labor force of HP, cut spending, and, if he had to buy growth in terms of an acquisition, he would do that as well. Hurd was obsessive about earnings, and Wall Street loved him for that. When the announcement of his departure came, the stock fell $4 per share, from $46 to $42. That's a $4 Mark Hurd premium on the stock.

What is an investor to do then? Step One would be to follow the institutions and cut back on your ownership in Hewlett-Packard immediately. But, let's assume that you are like me and you still like the hardware and services space. So while you want to be out of Hewlett-Packard, you still want to be in the sector. That's when I looked at IBM. Both HP and IBM are in the same markets, and when I did some due diligence on IBM, I saw a strong story there. I saw a stock that was building in confidence. I wanted the exposure to hardware and services, so I saw IBM as a great alternative to HP (see figures 8.4 and 8.5).

On August 9, IBM was trading at $129 per share, before the Hurd announcement. On November 9, three months later, IBM was trading at about $146 per share while Hewlett-Packard hadn't done anything. Staying in HP would have meant keeping dead money in the market. So what happened? The story changed and the momentum changed. Confidence was redistributed. The premium went from Hewlett-Packard into IBM in light of HP's revelations about Hurd. In essence, IBM benefitted from HP's bad news. IBM, under the leadership of CEO Sam Palmisano, was able to see where the business was going. He understood change, and so he was able to reposition IBM through innovation, emphasizing IBM's commitment to R&D and diversification, moving from hardware to services.

The challenge is to recognize that change—not three months out, but while it is happening or shortly thereafter. So if you were

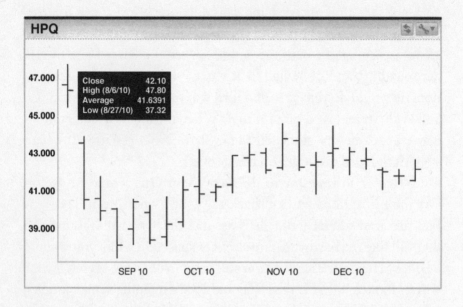

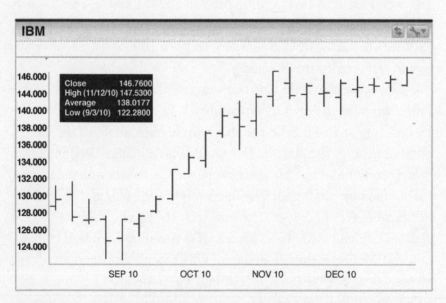

Figures 8.4 and 8.5: HP (above) and IBM Weekly Charts, September–
December 2010

an owner of HP, it doesn't mean you get out of the hardware services story, you just have to understand that the momentum is shifting, the story is changing, and the place for you to be is not in Hewlett-Packard but in IBM.

### Another Stealth Indicator: Short Interest

Another great measure of momentum and strength in a stock is something called "short interest." When measured as a percentage, short interest is simply the percent of a stock's outstanding shares that are held in short positions. In other words, it indicates the number of shares (or percentage of the stock) that people are betting will go down as opposed to the number of shares that are held as a long position. I believe that short interest is a phenomenal indicator, and it tells you what the sentiment is surrounding a particular security.

Once again, this is an easy statistic to find. On Yahoo! Finance, under "Company" and "Key Statistics" (on the left hand side of the screen), is listed both the number of "Shares Short" as well as the "Short % of Float." When you buy a stock or put one on your watch list, this statistic should be written in your notebook as one of the key indicators. And as you perform your due diligence from week to week, you should keep track of this percentage and note any change in this key percentage.

For example, let's say you buy Salesforce.com (CRM) on September 1 (the numbers that follow are for illustration only). When you buy the stock on September 1, you note that the stock has an "open interest" of 6 percent and the stock is trading at $110 per share. *Open interest* is the calculation, usually using futures and options contracts, of the number of open trades in a given market. It is an indication of strength. It is expressed as a percentage, and you should note that percentage in your notebook.

On September 15, you check back. The open interest has gone up to 7 percent, and the stock is trading at $115.

Now on October 15, the open interest is 10 percent, and the stock is trading at $128 (remember, you are recording all of these dates and changes in your notebook).

On November 1, the open interest is 11 percent, and the stock is trading at $140.

What you are looking for is both a rise in the stock price and an orderly increase in the amount of open interest on the stock. The moves do not need to be in lockstep (meaning the increases do not need to be percentage for percentage), but as long as both are moving up in an orderly manner, that is a bullish sign because increasing open interest generally is a sign of strength and confidence in the current price movement, and so it should give you great confidence to keep the position or add to it.

When open interest increases without a corresponding move in price, it tells you that more and more people don't believe in the stock. The shorts are adding to their positions. So, if we look back at the Salesforce.com example in which short interest appreciates with the stock price, it means that many traders are adding to their short positions, throwing good money after bad. They are in a bad position and are adding money to it. They are on the wrong side of the trade but can't recognize it or can't admit it. Either way, their pain in losing money is a bullish indicator, and one that I have great confidence in. It is one of the key indicators I look at before I pull the trigger on an asset.

As far as what percentage is an ideal percentage for open interest, I think that any time the percentage is above 8 percent, you are looking at a stock with great potential. And if short interest goes into double digits, your argument for owning that stock is strengthened that much more. If all of your other indicators line up, such as the earnings story and the technical story (e.g., the stock is trading above all three of its major moving averages), this is a stock that you should be in, and you should be in at an overweight position.

There is also the other side of the equation, and many investors (professional or otherwise) disagree with me on this point. If a stock's price is falling and the percentage of open interest also is falling, that's a stock I avoid. Many investors would say that this could be a great time to buy that stock, since it is pulling back and you can now get in at a better price point. But I do not agree with that thinking because it runs counter to the "buy high, sell higher" mind-set.

If the stock is falling along with open interest, the investors who are short are finally getting their way. The stock is falling, so the shorts are finally making money, but they are taking their money off the table too soon. They are getting out too soon. That's a situation in which institutions will exit or cut back their holdings, and you want to do the same.

9

# Invest in Commodities

Until the last decade, investors could do well by simply owning stocks and bonds. Today, however, increasing volatility in the U.S. and European markets coupled with the rise of BRICs has created an investing landscape where retail investors should consider adding currencies and commodities to their plans. Think of it this way: the S&P 500 delivered negative returns from 2000 to 2009, starting the decade at 1,455 and finishing at 1,115 at the end of 2009. During the same period the Goldman Sachs Commodity Index (GSCI) delivered a positive return, starting at 194.223 and ending at 524.61.

With numbers like those, it is easy to see why commodities like gold and oil have become an important part of the portfolios of most professionals. In addition, the energy sector has become a critical part of the S&P 500, and it is something I believe all investors should own, even if it constitutes only a small percentage of their portfolios (e.g., 10 to 20 percent). A lot of retail investors are intimidated by commodities; they picture them as volatile and complex. In this chapter, I'm going to demystify commodities and talk about some smart and safe strategies for investing in this asset class.

## Use Commodities as Alternatives to Stocks

If you would have asked someone at the beginning of 2000, when the NASDAQ was soaring to 5,000, where the best opportunity for growth would be for the coming decade, they likely would have answered Dell or Cisco Systems.

Dell (DELL), the company that defied all odds as a mail-order computer maker, emerged as a multi-billion-dollar success story (despite the fact that most investors believed that a mail-order computer company stood little chance of success). Dell was the number one stock of the 1990s, opening in January 1990 at 0.586 cents and closing at $51 in December 1999. However, after reaching a peak of about $60 per share in early 2000, it traded between $10 and $40 for much of the next decade.

Like Dell, Cisco Systems (CSCO), which produces what CEO John Chambers called the "plumbing of the Internet," was a high flier and a growth stock in the 1990s. However, after reaching a peak of $80 per share in 2000, Cisco spent much of the next decade trading between $10 and $30. No longer a growth stock, some may have considered Cisco a value stock, but for the most part they would have been wrong.

With 20/20 hindsight, we know that many hundreds of stocks like Dell and Cisco suffered similar fates as a result of the dot-com crash of 2000–02. Some alternatives to stocks, though, experienced record performance during the past decade. Gold was one of them.

At the dawn of the new millennium, when tech stocks were all the rage, few investors were thinking about gold, which started the 2000s at $290 an ounce and was marking record highs of $1850 an ounce by August, 2011. An investor could have bought gold, which was an asset that epitomized confidence, pretty much at any time during the past decade and made money (see figure 9.1).

By 2010, almost everyone who was holding gold was looking for a reason to ring the cash register and sell his holdings. These

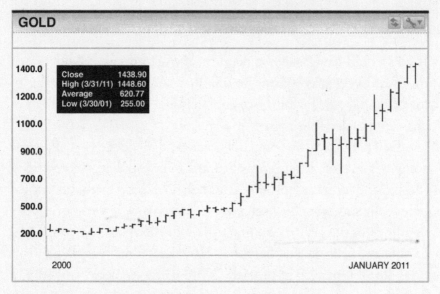

Figure 9.1: 10-Year Gold Chart, 2000–January 2011

days, people ask me all the time, "Should I get out of gold?" Although I think adjusting the size of one's holding in gold is fine, I do not recommend that investors get out of gold entirely. Gold is still a solid opportunity that allows investors to buy high and sell even higher. Between late January 2009 and July 2011, gold never traded below its 200-day moving average (see figure 9.2).

To remain above a security's 200-day moving average is seen as a bullish indicator, which is why the gold market is as structurally bullish as any you can find. Yet investors keep looking for reasons to exit the market. The reason behind this is twofold. For one, everyone seems to own gold, so it seems like an overly crowded trade (which means that because so many people own it, there is no shortage of investors who, at the first sign of trouble, will sell the precious metal, the precious metal ETF, or the commodity producer names). That initial price action often is the first sign that a bubble is about to pop. The other reason is that people who have profits in gold are looking for an excuse to cash them in.

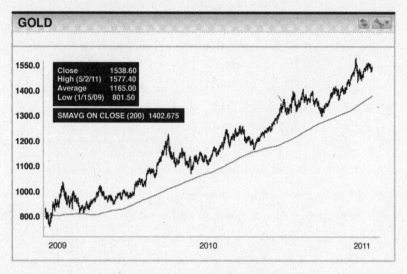

Figure 9.2: 2-Year Chart of Gold vs. its 200-Day Moving Average, January 2009–June 2011

## Focus on Metals and Energy

Gold is something that most investors can identify with, but other commodities can be intimidating to the average stock investor. This is generally the case for two reasons: the futures contracts used to trade them are not as intuitive as stocks, and the data needed to stay on top of "soft" commodities (think wheat, coffee, cocoa, and sugar) are not as readily available as information about stocks. That's why I recommend that the vast majority of individual investors focus their attention on energy and precious metals and avoid soft commodities.

Commodities are physical things—like grains, livestock, metals, and petroleum—that people need year-round. Today, even bandwidth, foreign currencies, and financial instruments are part of the commodity markets. Commodities require an active pool of buyers and sellers, and investors typically buy and sell commodities through futures contracts.

Commodities trade on commodity exchanges, such as the Chicago Mercantile Exchange, the Chicago Board of Trade, the Kansas City Board of Trade, and the New York Mercantile Exchange. Commodities exchanges, though, aren't limited to the United States, of course. Foreign exchanges include the Central Japan Commodity Exchange, the Hong Kong Mercantile Exchange, and Europe's NYSE Liffe.

The typical stock investor probably should think twice about investing in futures. For those investors who are wary of futures, commodities can be added to portfolios by investing in those companies whose business is related to commodities. Some commodity ETFs also offer paths into this space. Regardless of which way you decide to incorporate commodities into your portfolio, it's important to look beyond stocks to this important investment vehicle.

## Turning Insights into Investments

Investors certainly should not be afraid to look beyond stocks to other investment opportunities. Commodities are one option I endorse—with a caveat. Overall, commodities can be tricky investments, especially for everyday investors who typically focus on equities. In 2008, most people invested in commodities because they were going up. But most investors didn't really understand why. They didn't understand what was going on fundamentally and what was changing in the world. But they did view commodities as potentially becoming a winning asset class. As a result, everyone scrambled, particularly on the institutional side, to offer alternative investment products, and most turned to commodities. They called them "alternative investments" and "diversification tools," and they dressed them up with sexy names, but they were nothing more than commodities. People fell in love with them.

Diversifying your portfolio is all well and good, but you need to understand what you're investing in. The problem with pushing commodities in 2008 was that they were uncorrelated to the rest of the broad market. When the credit crisis hit, the world got a global margin call. When the world gets a global margin call, everything correlates to one—that is, everything moves in the same direction—and in this case it was down. Basically, everyone lost a tremendous amount of money.

Now, in 2011, the commodities market has returned, and more investors understand the need to invest in commodities. Investors are better educated and understand that commodities can help them tap into the benefits of the industrialization of the emerging world, the rising up of a new middle class.

Think about it. Why wouldn't you protect yourself against the rising cost of food, energy, health care, and technology? Those are all the things that the rising middle class in the emerging world wants. Today, investors are better educated than they were just a few years ago. Savvy investors know that there is a really nice selection of potential alternative investments in the form of commodities, especially when it comes to energy and precious metals. Wall Street very likely will soon create products—not just in energy or precious metals, but in food products, agricultural products, cotton products, fabric products, sugar, coffee, soybeans, wheat, and uranium—that will help investors look beyond stocks. In the meantime, what is a straightforward way to turn your thoughts about where the world is headed into an investing strategy? Energy.

## Energy and the Emerging Economies

I have some pretty strong feelings about specific commodities. In fact, I have always considered one part of the commodity space to tower above the others in order of importance. That commodity is energy. In recent years, I have always kept some energy in my portfolio, usually at market weight or, more often, at overweight.

Energy, which includes such things as coal, gas, and oil, powers so much of our lives, here in the United States and around the globe. Energy is, of course, a natural resource that comes from only certain parts of the world. However, the need for energy knows no borders. Even though the bulk of oil and oil-related products comes from only a handful of countries, dozens of countries consistently import significant amounts of oil, natural gas, and other energy-related commodities.

My former boss, Mark Fisher, has said that "energy and crude oil are the ultimate currency." The demand for oil and its many by-products shows no signs of slowing down. Take China, for example. China has one of the fastest-growing economies in the world, and it has the second-largest economy (after the United States). We know that Chinese officials are trying to get their hands on as many barrels of oil as they can. They also are looking to acquire the actual physical assets surrounding the production of oil. They do this via many joint ventures (many of which are with Russia), which tells us a great deal about their appetite for oil and energy by-products.

Unlike China, the United States has a significant advantage over most other countries because it maintains a stockpile of oil in the Strategic Petroleum Reserve (SPR). According to the U.S. Department of Energy, the SPR is the largest supply of emergency crude oil on the planet. Located in enormous underground salt caverns in Louisiana, the reserves are almost always filled to capacity at 727 million barrels of oil. (In the United States, the president decides when to release any of those millions of barrels.)

I point out the SPR to demonstrate the potential for increased demand by other countries that are striving to be as prepared for an emergency as the United States. While the United States remains, by far, the largest importer of oil (it imported about nine million barrels of oil a day in 2009), China has surpassed Japan to become the second-largest oil importer (followed by Japan, Germany, India, and South Korea). In fact, China already has developed its own strategic oil reserve. But it still has a long way to go before it will complete its plans for stockpiling its oil reserve. The Chinese are developing their government-controlled reserve in three phases.

The first phase called for the preserving of just over 100 million barrels of oil, and that first part of the plan was largely completed by the end of 2008. The second phase is slated to preserve an additional 170 million barrels of oil and is expected to be completed in 2011. And the last phase calls for an additional 204 million barrels of oil by 2020. That is just China's plan. Many other countries will be following in America's and China's footsteps in the years ahead, which will create even more demand for oil and other by-products of oil. The demand for energy isn't going away anytime soon.

I believe that investors should incorporate energy into their own portfolios (most often at market weight or overweight). Why? Energy often is a relatively strong investment and often can be used as a hedge against inflation.

To illustrate the relative strength of energy in recent years, I will use the company Exxon Mobil (XOM)—the largest corporation in the world in terms of market capitalization (stock market worth)—as an example. Remember that although commodities typically are traded in the futures markets, investors also can invest in the stocks of those companies that focus on commodities.

So, let's look at the performance of Exxon during the height of the financial crisis. In October 2008, the month after the Lehman Brothers bankruptcy, you could have bought Exxon Mobil for a price below $55 per share. As the markets continued to plummet through the rest of 2008, Exxon moved higher, to a point just above $80 per share (see figure 9.3).

What explains Exxon's strength while the vast majority of stocks were losing their value? Money managers decided that regardless of overall market conditions, they still wanted some exposure to energy. Put another way, even in the worst of times, asset managers still want to have some energy in their portfolios. So what were they doing? They were moving out of high-risk

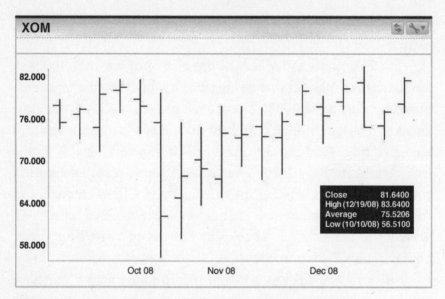

Figure 9.3: Exxon Mobil, September 5, 2008–January 2, 2009

names in the oil services, drilling, and refining spaces (as well as weaker energy stocks) and instead focusing on the one company that had the strongest balance sheet in the industry: Exxon. Even though Armageddon was coming, they reasoned, we will own energy through the biggest company in the world, the best balance sheet in the world, and the company that had the most proven reserves in the world. And that was Exxon Mobil. This is a textbook example of why owning energy at all times is a sound investing strategy and one that I have always lived by.

The other advantage to owning energy is that it is a good hedge against inflation. In essence, you're protecting yourself against the competitiveness of the rest of the world. As emerging countries like China and Brazil become more advanced, some of their home-grown companies may become threats to certain U.S. companies. However, the one thing these other countries will always need is energy, which is why global demand for energy is likely to remain strong for years to come. As a result, even in an environment of rising interest rates, when most stocks usually fare poorly, energy is likely to continue to appreciate.

When we talk about the emerging economies, an important metric to keep your eye on is how much money it will require to bring these countries into the twenty-first century. It is estimated that by the year 2030, $65 trillion will be spent on industrializing emerging economies. That includes improvement in infrastructure, goods and services, transportation and energy, power sources, and so forth.

The BRIC countries—Brazil, Russia, India, and China— have been acknowledged as the four key emerging economies of the world. However, economist Jim O'Neill at Goldman Sachs, who coined the term *BRIC* in 2001, has said that eleven other nations also likely will play a major role as they industrialize and grow.

Africa is one of those areas poised for growth. In fact, in December 2010, South Africa formally joined the BRIC nations (now known as BRICS) as one of the world's emerging economic powers. But beyond just the country of South Africa, the entire continent of Africa has yet to be fully developed. In order for Africa to industrialize, one of the main things local governments and businesses will need is energy. Africa and other developing nations—and the energy needs that will arise out of the growth of those nations—are one of the key reasons I urge investors to take a long view of energy and get exposure to energy in their portfolios. However, I have very specific techniques that I suggest investors use in order to get that exposure to energy.

What I do not recommend to investors is to purchase any investing vehicle that is directly tied to the price of oil. Unless you are a professional oil trader, that's the wrong way to approach this market. Given the great volatility of the oil market, you don't want to get up every morning having to worry about the spot price of oil. Instead, individual investors should understand two key principles: contango and backwardization.

## Contango and Backwardization

Here is the part of the chapter that may have some investors rolling their eyes, but it is crucial for investors to understand why I recommend that they avoid oil ETFs and other investments that are directly tied to the price of oil. The only way to do that is to explain two concepts that sound more like mathematics or physics terms rather than investing principles. Those terms are *contango* and *backwardization*.

Contango and backwardization are opposites. The terms come from the relationship between short-dated and long-dated futures contracts. The best way to explain this is through an example.

Remember that most commodities are traded directly through the futures markets. Futures contracts are forward-looking, exchange-traded contracts. So, let's say that a barrel of oil is priced at $93 for next month. Let's also assume that the price for that same commodity is at $97 per barrel twelve months from now. When the future price of oil is higher and the slope of the futures curve is upward, that is called contango (see figure 9.4). When there is contango, which is a fairly common market condition, prices get progressively higher in future delivery months. Contango can be used to describe the forward slope of any futures contract.

Let's turn the tables and look at the reverse situation. Backwardization is when the price of a commodity is lower in the distant delivery months than it is in the delivery months in the near future. It is the opposite of contango. So, in our example, backwardization would be when the price of silver is worth $35.70 per troy ounce one month from now and $34.80 per troy ounce four years from now, as shown in figure 9.5.

In a contango market, investors believe that the price of a commodity will rise in the coming months, and that there is no near-term supply challenge or disruption. A backwardization market indicates that there is a near-term supply challenge or disruption.

Here is the investment problem: when you invest in a pure oil

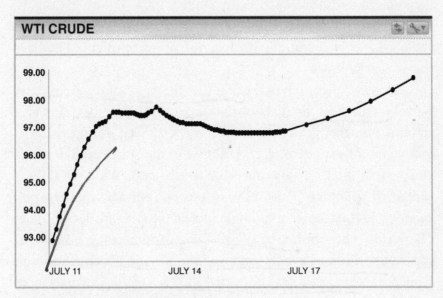

Figure 9.4: Contango Example Using Oil

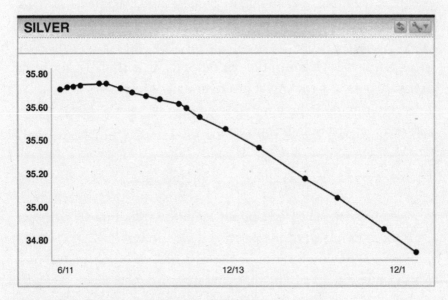

Figure 9.5: Backwardization Slope for Silver

ETF, one that is specifically trying to track the underlying price of a commodities future, such as the United States Oil Fund (USO), you expose yourself to the contango-backwardization effect. If the market is in contango, that means that every month, you have to pay to stay invested.

Let me explain. Hypothetically, if the price of oil is $100 per barrel in the first month, but the price is $112 per barrel twelve months out, the difference is $12. If everything during the next twelve months is equal, you are going to pay an extra $12 just to stay in that oil ETF investment. That's because what the ETF is doing every month is rolling the futures contract from the first month into the second month, the second into the third, and so on. (Basically, when an investor "rolls" a futures contract, he is selling one position before its maturity and buying another one with a longer maturity.) That means that they are paying a dollar more each month and passing that cost along to the holders of the ETF. That's why investors should avoid pure energy ETFs so that they are not susceptible to contango or backwardization effects.

A natural gas ETF such as the United States Natural Gas Fund (UNG) is vulnerable to the same contango and backwardization issues as oil. That's one of the reasons why, in early 2011, the price of natural gas was trading at just over half of its 52-week high. It's a depreciating asset because you continually have to factor in the cost of a forward rolling contract.

## A Better Way to Play Energy

Now you know why I do not advocate the use of an oil or other ETF directly linked to the price of the underlying asset. I simply do not want any investor to bet on the price of oil or natural gas. That's more like gambling than investing. So what is the best way to rack up profits in the energy sector?

Investing in top energy companies is very different from investing in an oil or energy ETF. Most investors can't handle the fluctuations of the price of energy like professional oil traders can. Futures contracts in oil also likely aren't the best investing methods for most individual investors. Instead, the best way for individuals to invest in energy is to invest in the profitability of energy companies based on global demand and pricing power. So which companies make the best investments?

The best investments are not the companies that own the actual barrels of oil, but the companies that own everything that is needed to get those barrels of oil out of the ground. This means oil service companies, drillers, refiners—the entire oil space. I want investors to become owners—that is, shareholders—of these companies.

Does this mean that there are no energy ETFs worth investing in? The answer is no. Two energy ETFs are worthy of every investor's consideration. They are Oil Services Holders (OIH) and the Energy SPDR (XLE), both of which we've mentioned in earlier chapters. The key to both of these ETFs is that neither is linked or tracked to the price of oil.

OIH includes oil service names such as Schlumberger (SLB), Transocean (RIG), and Halliburton (HAL), which in early 2011 were the three biggest holdings of that ETF (see table 9.1). I recommend that an investor take a close look at the OIH ETF or consider owning a few of the top names in this ETF. To figure out which would be the best investment (i.e., owning the ETF or owning the top stocks of the ETF individually), an investor needs to do his due diligence (e.g., look at the moving averages, get a sense of the volume and momentum, etc.).

The other energy ETF that is worthy of analysis is XLE. This ETF has about forty holdings of the top integrated energy names in the industry. In early 2011, as you can see from table 9.2, the three biggest names in the ETF are Exxon (XOM), Chevron (CVX), and ConocoPhillips (COP). I want to reiterate that this ETF is also a potential winner because it holds the actual energy companies, none of which is directly linked to the price of oil.

### Table 9.1: OIH Holdings

| Stock | Symbol |
| --- | --- |
| Schlumberger N.V. | SLB |
| Transocean Ltd. | RIG |
| Halliburton Co. | HAL |
| Baker Hughes Inc. | BHI |
| Diamond Offshore Drilling Inc. | DO |
| National Oilwell Varco Inc. | NOV |
| Noble Corporation | NE |
| Cameron International Corp. | CAM |
| Weatherford International Ltd. | WFT |
| Nabors Industries Inc. | NBR |
| Ensco Plc. | ESV |
| Tidewater Inc. | TDW |
| Rowan Companies Inc. | RDC |
| Exterran Holdings Inc. | EXH |

Source: ETF Investment Outlook

### Table 9.2: XLE Holdings

| Stock | Symbol |
| --- | --- |
| Exxon Mobil Corp. | XOM |
| Chevron Corp. | CVX |
| ConocoPhillips | COP |
| Schlumberger N.V. | SLB |
| Occidental Petroleum Corp. | OXY |
| Devon Energy Corp. | DVN |
| Apache Corp. | APA |
| Anadarko Petroleum Corp. | APC |
| Marathon Oil Corp. | MRO |
| Halliburton Co. | HAL |
| EOG Resources Inc. | EOG |
| Hess Corp. | HES |

| Stock | Symbol |
|---|---|
| Southwestern Energy Co. | SWN |
| National Oilwell Varco Inc. | NOV |
| Baker Hughes Inc. | BHI |
| Chesapeake Energy Corp. | CHK |
| Spectra Energy Corp. | SE |
| Murphy Oil Corp. | MUR |
| Noble Energy Inc. | NBL |
| Williams Cos. | WMB |
| Valero Energy Corp. | VLO |
| Peabody Energy Corp. | BTU |
| El Paso Corp. | EP |
| CONSOL Energy Inc. | CNX |
| Diamond Offshore Drilling Inc. | DO |
| Cameron International Corp. | CAM |
| Range Resources Corp. | RRC |
| ENSCO Plc. | ESV |
| Nabors Industries Inc. | NBR |
| Pioneer Natural Resources Co. | PXD |
| Cabot Oil & Gas Corp. | COG |
| Rowan Cos. Inc. | RDC |
| Sunoco Inc. | SUN |
| Tesoro Corp. | TSO |
| FMC Technologies Inc. | FTI |
| Denbury Resources Inc. | DNR |

*Source: ETF Investment Outlook*

Again, the simplest way to play the energy space would be to buy one of these ETFs. (Other choices might include Vanguard's VGENX fund or Fidelity's FSENX fund, both of which include similar energy-related stocks.) Even though I generally am not the biggest fan of ETFs, OIH and XLE are the exceptions to the rule and are worthy of consideration for individual investors. Another option, as mentioned, would be for investors to investigate the top holdings in these two ETFs to see whether they would be appropriate fits for their portfolios. For investors who aren't particularly keen on investing in commodities via futures contracts, investing in commodity-based ETFs or individual energy stocks might be a suitable alternative.

When it comes to looking beyond stocks, commodities can provide individual investors with a suitable alternative investment vehicle that may boost alpha and work as a hedge. This is particularly true when talking about energy and precious metals because these sectors don't require opening futures accounts, a type of trading better left to the pros. Instead, investors can get exposure to commodities by investing in companies that focus on energy and precious metals. Commodity ETFs offer another avenue into this space without having to trade in the futures markets. Regardless of the route you take into the commodities space, though, it is crucial that you understand what you're investing in. Don't get caught up in the noise. Discuss your approach with your team to ensure that whichever commodities tactic you employ fits with your overall investing plan.

# Conclusion

Professional investors create strategies and stick to their plans. They do their homework. They work with their teams. They know how to keep emotions from taking over their investing. However, even the most level-headed investor can find himself in a bad place every once in a while. What I want to leave you with is a way to get out of a slump when you have the misfortune of hitting one.

It takes a healthy head to generate healthy returns. So how do you get yourself out of the penalty box? At MBF, when we saw that a trader was about to go on a bad streak, we would tell him to take some time off. To go spend some money. We would give him permission to forget about the market and be selfish. We knew that spending some money and enjoying some quality time would help him regain his focus—and reacquire an understanding of the value of a dollar, and respect it.

My team did the same thing for me in September 2009.

After my uncle's aneurysm, I felt lost, angry, and orphaned. I was trading recklessly. Someone needed to pay for my uncle's tragedy, so I decided to pick a fight with the market. Guess who won?

How out of my mind was I? I'm a huge football fan, and I hadn't even realized that the season had started. That's how out of touch I was. I was at a critical point in my life. Had I kept trying to work through my anger, grief, and sadness through ill-conceived trades, I could have lost everything I had worked so hard to achieve that year. My team helped me realize that I needed to take some time out.

So I cut down my positions and wouldn't allow myself to put on any new trades. My daily routine for Virtus and *Fast Money* did not change; but instead of executing plays as a quarterback, I stood on the sidelines with the clipboard in my hand and watched the game. The only solution was to follow the same advice I had given to so many other traders over the years: I needed to do something for myself.

For some investors, being selfish means buying a new fully-loaded Porsche or heading to the Bahamas for a week of deep-sea fishing. To me, being selfish meant getting a dog—and not just any dog, but my very own dog. I have had many pet dogs in my lifetime, but all of them were dogs that my family had selected: my childhood poodle; our current French bulldog, Tonka. During my time away from the market, I decided that I was going to select my own dog. I did the research and found a breeder in Pennsylvania that had been breeding yellow Labs for thirty years. I wanted a yellow Lab because to me it is the quintessential "man's best friend." I was scheduled to pick him up on October 8, 2009.

October 8 was a sunny, beautiful Thursday. The air was crisp with just a little bite of fall to it. The MLB playoff series had started the night before, and, unlike the NFL opening in September, I was focused on every pitch while watching the Yankees take on the Twins. Most important, it was the day I would head to Hershey Dale Kennels in Shippensburg, Pennsylvania, to pick up my new yellow lab, Timber. My main focus that day was Timber and the Yankees victory the night before. The market, which normally would be front and center in my mind, was really an afterthought. In hindsight, that was exactly what my time away was supposed to do: place life in perspective. And on October 8, I knew I had done just that.

"Time away" did not mean I had completely tuned out the market. I watched the markets and continued to formulate investment ideas. But I didn't implement those ideas yet. For instance, during my three weeks in the penalty box, I had been keeping my eye on gold and oil. During September, gold made a breakout move to the upside. Curiously, crude oil did not break out in September along with gold, trading in a sideways range. But I was confident that crude oil was about to make a similar breakout move. I noticed that on the last day of September, crude jumped from $66.22 to $70.61. Crude was on my radar.

Though what was happening with crude oil had captured my interest, I was really just focused on meeting Timber. My good friend, Pete, drove us that morning and he couldn't drive fast enough to the farm in Pennsylvania. But something about that morning—maybe it was the recognition that I had regained my perspective—gave me the confidence that I was ready to get back in the market. The clouds that had been hanging over my head cleared. I knew from my years of managing traders that my first step back should be gentle, slow, and modest. Just test the waters. So instead of buying, let's say, 1,000 shares, I decided on 200 shares. While in the car on the way to Pennsylvania, I placed a trade to buy the XLE right on the open at $55 (as you'll remember, XLE is the energy ETF we discussed in depth in chapter 9). But then, driving through the mountains to this breeder's remote farm, I lost cell phone reception. I was disconnected from the world for a good five hours. Guess what? It didn't matter. I wasn't even thinking about the markets.

The next morning, after a fun evening of watching Yankee baseball and horsing around with my new dog, I began to prepare for *Fast Money*. I checked in on the markets and noticed that oil had jumped from the previous day's opening of $69.50 to above $72. Obviously the XLE moved higher as well, from $55 to $56.60. I chuckled to myself, happy in the knowledge that I had my perspective back.

Some time away and a yellow lab named Timber had sprung me from the penalty box. I had seen this moment happen to other investors many times during my twenty years in the business, and now it was my turn. I knew this moment was a turning point. I knew I was okay. I could still ride the bicycle. I sized the position right. I listened to my team. I got my emotions back in order. I was confident again, and I knew that it was time to get back into the markets.

\* \* \*

The foundation for successful investing is built upon a proper mental framework. Success requires thinking, acting, and feeling like a professional. After reading this book, you will naturally want to execute like a professional. However, trying to do so—especially in today's fast-moving markets—without having clarity of thought is nearly impossible.

The financial markets have changed dramatically during the past ten years. Today, the markets are still evolving. We are in a state of transition, somewhere between buy-and-hold investing and the high-speed momentum trading practiced by a handful of professional investors. Volatility is here to stay, and events like the Flash Crash are permanent fixtures in our markets. As a result, investors today can't approach the market the same way they did a decade ago. The precipitous decline from September 2008 to March 2009 could happen again. And unfortunately, when these market gyrations occur, they will happen even faster than they have in the past. Witness the week of August 8, 2011. On Monday the Dow had an intraday price swing of 625 points—on Tuesday 640, Wednesday 542, and Thursday 549. That's why investors need to accept this new investing landscape rather than fear it and embrace buying high and selling higher.

In the end what does buying high and selling higher mean to me? It means finding stocks where price, volume, and momentum tell me that there is visible confidence in that stock as opposed to the traditional model of buying value stocks whose prices are falling yet fail to exhibit any signs of visible confidence.

As you begin your career as a "buy high, sell higher" investor, it's important to have role models. Who specifically should you emulate? If you're a retail investor, look to the professional and institutional investing techniques that I have outlined in this book. But as you attempt to execute like a pro, it's important for you to recognize your own strengths and your own risk tolerance. As discussed throughout this book, I believe that the habits of professional investors and institutional investors should be studied very closely by retail investors. If you are an individual investor, you should try to do the same things that professional investors do every day. You try to approach the markets and execute like a professional trader or investor. But you must do this within your own abilities, which means playing to your own individual strengths.

Now that you've read this book, you have some of the same tools at your disposal to spot a stock, bond, or commodity that is exuding confidence, the ways the top investors do. But the final element that separates good amateur investors from the Hall of Fame–worthy pros is the psychological piece of the puzzle. You need to have your mental state under control. You need to neutralize emotion and ego. You need to understand your own personal limitations.

Warren Buffett talks about holding stocks "forever." Most people can't do that. In fact, most investors shouldn't do that. Unless you've got the same bank balance as Buffett, "the Oracle of Omaha," you can't afford to invest the way he does. Think about it: he was playing offense during that grim September of

2008—buying upward of $5 billion of preferred shares of Goldman Sachs at a $115 strike price—while most investors were at best liquidating their portfolios. That's why no one should invest like Buffett (even though there has been a cottage industry of "how to invest like Buffett" books published since the 1990s).

Realistically, Main Street—that is, average retail investors—really can't buy and hold. Nor does Main Street have the time or skills to day-trade. So if you spend your investment time trying to be something other than yourself, it will never work for you. Success in investing is measured by your ability to capitalize on your strengths and on your ability to achieve alpha (extra or outsized returns). That's what institutional investors do: they are always looking for alpha. That's why you are not only taking a hard, long look at the market; you are taking a hard, long look at yourself as well.

During my early career as an investor and trader, I spent too much time trying to be something that I wasn't, trying to be a certain type of trader that I just didn't have the capabilities to be. When you try to be something you aren't, you waste time and you waste talent. So rather than try to be a trader who swings for the fences trying to rack up returns of 20 to 30 percent per year, it makes much more sense to try to be an investor who earns a steady 5 to 10 percent per year. One easy way to improve your performance is to skip the latest fads or financial products, particularly if you don't understand them. If you don't have the time to research all the components in a mortgage-backed security, skip it. Let another guy make a killing with them. If the explanation of a Master Limited Partnership makes your head spin, you know what? There are other ways to get oil, gas, and transportation into your portfolio.

In the new investing landscape, there is no such thing as a free lunch—or a risk-free 7 percent return. Institutions and professional investors spend their lives keeping abreast of the financial markets. They spend their lives being on top of the market. Most retail investors can't allocate that much time to studying the markets, but they can't be lazy, either. They have to do their homework. Most individual investors really need to devote more time to the markets if they are going to be successful. But there is some middle ground; not eighty hours per week like professional traders, but perhaps fifteen to twenty hours a week will be all individual investors need to make good investment decisions. But investors can't rely solely on the research of others. Like my good friend CNBC's Gary Kaminsky says, "When you rely on the research of others, you only know what they know. You don't know what they don't know."

I also believe strongly that there is no place for huge egos in investing. If you approach the markets with humility, you have a far greater chance for success than you do when you approach the market with ego. Ego is the enemy. People don't understand that. People remember *Wall Street* (the first movie), and they love to quote Gordon Gekko's advice that "greed is good." I think Gekko is wrong. Greed is not necessarily good, but confidence is.

Instead, you have to treat the market with great respect. You constantly have to ask yourself, "Where am I wrong?" That's really what the market is about. One should not approach the market with the question, "How much money can I make?" That's not approaching the market with respect. The real questions are "Where am I wrong?" and "How much can I lose?" That's the way professional investors approach the market. They protect the downside first. If you solve the "Where am I wrong?" component of it, then you'll be okay.

Speaking of "How much can I lose?" another thing to be wary of as you begin your career as a "buy high, sell higher" investor is what Wall Street pundits mean when they talk about being diversified. Don't let diversification give you false confidence, because when a black swan event comes around, every sector and multiple asset class may come tumbling down. Too many so-called experts claim that if you're diversified, you don't have to worry about where you're wrong. That's simply not true. It's a fallacy because black swan events do happen. And when they do, it's always going to be Main Street, the passive investor, that's told to hang in there. And that is why retail investors lose the most money when markets tank.

Experts who preach the message of "hang in there" don't understand that the guy on Main Street doesn't have the stomach or the fortitude or the resources of the professional investor. He doesn't have it within himself to strip the emotion out and not make the wrong decision in times of peril. So if you look back, history will always show that the black swans appear. If you think back to the credit crisis and October 2008, one of the reasons why I knew in my gut that the markets would continue to plummet was because the market was going lower in such an aggressive fashion. I'd seen that before. I've seen the biggest and the best be placed in that position, and when the market moves that fast, it's so difficult to figure out what to do. Few people can make correct decisions in the midst of a market meltdown when emotions are running high.

One example that illustrates why retail investors lose the most money during big market events can be traced back to Columbus Day, 2008. On that day in October, the Dow surged by more than 900 points. I knew that it was a false rally, as did so many professional and institutional investors. That was why I used that day to get out of many of the positions I had been holding. I used it as an opportunity to sell a number of holdings that I believed would go lower in the days and weeks ahead. And I know of a number of professional traders and institutional investors who also lightened up on their portfolios that same day, moving from overweight or market weight to underweight.

What about the retail investor? He or she likely saw this huge surge as the beginning of a bull market. Retail investors were not selling into this rally. Like during so many other key market events, retail investors were the last to get it right.

But things are changing. Retail investors are no longer looking only to blue-chip stocks to lock in profits. Instead, they are looking for growth wherever they can find it. In fact, right now, I see the entire nation of investors in the United States attempting to redefine our situation. We are not only redefining how we invest, we are redefining where our growth as a country is likely to come from. This will change the investing landscape for years to come, and the investors who will come out ahead are those willing to roll up their sleeves, ask questions, challenge the status quo, be active, and arm themselves with the same tools that institutional investors use every day, the ones that I discussed throughout this book.

The interesting thing is that these tools—such as checking price and volume against 50-, 100-, and 200-day moving averages—are actually very easy to find and use. However, it is important to not be sucked into all of the noise coming from Wall Street. The Wall Street experts I see on television and being quoted in the media usually don't point investors in the right direction. The mistake that many of these so-called experts make is that they don't identify for the viewer or reader that there are social consequences and market consequences associated with different events. But while the social consequence of a particular condition may not be favorable for Main Street, the market consequence might be quite favorable for stock prices to rise.

What I believe my colleagues on *Fast Money* do exceptionally well is highlight the differences between social consequences and emphasize what the market consequences are. For example, in August 2010, Ben Bernanke suggested the possibility of a second round of quantitative easing to help the troubled financial markets. Main Street took that as a sign that the dollar was going to be cheapened and that the standard of living would fall. They were right. That was the social consequence. But the market consequence was that risky asset classes were all going to rise because the dollar was going to cheapen.

\* \* \*

When you assess your participation in the market, you have to ask yourself a couple of tough questions: "Do I belong in the market financially and emotionally?" "Do I have the knowledge necessary to be in the market?" It's not about getting rich or staying rich. It's about you. It's about availing yourself of the tools, data, and information that you need to succeed. It's about growing and maturing as an investor. That's where your focus should be.

All markets go through multiple cycles, both domestically and globally. The markets will go through periods of higher appreciation and declining asset values. That's the reality of the markets. But the more knowledge you gain by doing all of the things that I recommend in this book, the better your chances of success.

As we know, all investors bring their own unique strengths and weaknesses to the market. That is why I contend that at the end of the day, your ability to adapt is one of the most important qualities you can have as an investor. After failing as a pit trader I did just that. I reinvented myself into the investor I am today. I've hung out with top investors. I've seen the best traders in action. And, as I've said, ego and an absence of respect for the market are two of the greatest enemies any investor could have.

I'm comfortable with who I am. I'm not a billionaire. I don't measure success in my life by the amount of zeroes in my bank account. Unfortunately, that is how most people on Wall Street measure their success. I measure success by my own personal yardstick: Am I maturing as an investor? Am I growing as a person? Within that context, I am as happy as I've ever been. That's why I always say the two most important things in life are health and happiness, because if you're not healthy, and you don't focus on attempting to be healthy, you have no place in the market. And I don't just mean physical health; I'm also talking about mental health. Make sure you understand this before going into the markets. If you don't agree that health and happiness are the two most important things in life, the chances are that you will never be anything more than a frustrated investor. Health and happiness: the two best positions in life. I wish that for all of you.

# Appendix

**Sample Investing Calendar plus
Supporting Commentary**

## VIRTUS
INVESTMENT PARTNERS

## Is Red the Color of February?

Joe Terranova, Chief Market Strategist, Virtus Investment Partners, offers insights into some of the key economic indicators and meaningful market events to keep a close eye on throughout February.

**February 2011**

| Sunday | Monday | Tuesday | Wednesday | Thursday | Friday | Saturday |
|---|---|---|---|---|---|---|
| | | **1**<br>10:00 AM: **ISM Manufacturing Index** (January)<br>**Domestic Motor Vehicle Sales** (January) | **2** | **3**<br>Chinese New Year Begins | **4**<br>8:30 AM:<br>**Private Sector Jobs and U.S. Unemployment Report** (January) | **5** |
| **6** | **7** | **8** | **9**<br>1:00 PM:<br>10-Yr T-Note Auction | **10**<br>1:00 PM:<br>30-Yr T-Bond Auction | **11** | **12** |
| **13** | **14** | **15**<br>**Treasury's GSE Reform Report Due Mid-Month**<br>8:30 AM:<br>**Retail Sales** (January) | **16**<br>8:30 AM: **Housing Starts** (January)<br>9:15 AM: **Industrial Production** (January) | **17**<br>8:30 AM:<br>**CPI**<br>(January) | **18** | **19** |
| **20** | **21** | **22** | **23**<br>10:00 AM:<br>**Existing Home Sales** (January) | **24**<br>8:30 AM:<br>**Durable Goods Orders** (January) | **25**<br>8:30 AM: **GDP** (Q4p)<br>9:00 AM:<br>**S&P/Case-Shiller HPI** (December) | **26** |
| **27** | **28**<br>**Will the Fed Respond Early to Banks' Capital Plans?**<br>9:00 PM:<br>**China PMI** (February) | | | | | |

*Times shown are Eastern Standard (EST).*

Historically, no news is good news in February. In fact, red is the color of Valentine's Day, Chinese New Year – and a declining market for the last four Februarys: the major sell-off of February 27, 2007, the sideways market of February 2008, losses throughout February 2009, and the early February decline of 2010. Will 2011 make five red Februarys in a row? The first week, highlighted by ISM manufacturing and unemployment data, should hint at whether red will be the color of February this year or not.

## February indicators / events of note:

### ISM Manufacturing Index

The Institute of Supply Management issues its January report on February 1. This influential monthly measure of the health of U.S. manufacturing is based on an in-depth survey of 300 manufacturing firms. An index value of 50 is the dividing line between an expanding or slowing economy.

### Domestic Motor Vehicle Sales

U.S. motor vehicle sales are an important component of consumer spending, and this monthly report, which is based on data from auto makers, indicates the direction of the economy. Data includes sales of domestically produced cars and light duty trucks. January sales data will be released on February 1.

### Chinese New Year Begins

Chinese New Year is the most important Chinese holiday. February 3 marks the start of the Year of the Rabbit, in particular the "golden rabbit," which is auspicious for wealth.

### Private Sector Jobs & U.S. Unemployment Report

On February 4, the January release of private payroll data is an important part of the monthly U.S. Employment Situation report issued by the Labor Department. This data gives the true employment story, is the best gauge of the economy's direction, and has the power to move markets.

### Treasury Auctions for:

> 10-year Treasury Notes on February 9
> 30-year Treasury Bonds on February 10

## You should be watching:

GE's recent earnings highlighted the strength of the industrial manufacturing sector, which has been growing at a healthy pace over the last few months. December ISM was 57. The market expects January ISM to also come in strong, around 57-58, which could help prevent a February correction. This report could set the tone for the month ahead.

Motor vehicle sales have shown the resiliency of the global and U.S. consumer. In January, U.S. motor vehicle sales rose to an annual rate of about 12.5 million units for domestic-made and imported vehicles combined, of which 9.4 million were domestics alone. In February, we'd like to see the annual unit rate rise above 12.6 million for domestics/imports and 9.55 million for domestics only. We would not like to see those numbers fall below previous levels of 12.53 million for domestics/imports total and 9.56 million for domestics alone.

China typically enters a shut-down phase of sorts over the 15-day Chinese New Year holiday period. In light of growing concern over China's overheated economy, it will be interesting to see what impact, if any, the protracted holiday has on the country's economic situation.

The unemployment rate fell to 9.4% in January, but the expectation for February is that it ticks back up to around 9.5%. January's headline number disappointed with only 103,000 jobs added, and we're looking for that number to come in at 125,000 to 135,000 for February. Private sector jobs came in at 113,000 last month; this month we're looking to add 140,000 to 150,000 private sector jobs.

U.S. Treasury yields have continued to rise through the early part of the year. If we see any signs of red in early February, whether from the ISM manufacturing index, unemployment report, and/or China's economic situation, watch to see if investors start to return to safe-haven assets. Treasury yields would be one of the early indicators to monitor.

Return to Page 1

Return to Page 1

## February indicators / events of note:

**Treasury's GSE Reform Report Revised Deadline**

Mid-February replaced January 31 as the deadline for the Treasury Department's GSE reform report. The GSEs (Government-Sponsored Enterprises) are a group of financial corporations such as Fannie Mae and Freddie Mac, created by Congress to enhance the flow of credit to the agriculture and home finance sectors of the economy.

**Retail Sales**

Retail sales data is released monthly by the U.S. Department of Commerce. January data will be released on February 15. Retail sales measure total receipts for sales of durable and nondurable goods. Consumer spending accounts for two-thirds of GDP and is therefore a key element in economic growth.

**Housing Starts**

The Commerce Department's monthly housing starts report is the most closely followed report on the housing sector because it discloses the number of new residential buildings under construction in the U.S. January's report is released on February 16.

**Industrial Production**

This monthly release by the U.S. Federal Reserve shows how much factories, mines, and utilities are producing – and how much factory capacity is in use. This data is an important measure of current output for the economy and helps to define turning points in the business cycle, such as the start of a recession or a recovery. January data is released on February 16.

**Consumer Price Index (CPI)**

CPI measures the price of goods and services paid by consumers, which makes it a key indicator of inflation. January CPI data will be released on February 17.

**Existing Home Sales**

This monthly report from the National Association of Realtors provides sales-closing data on previously constructed homes, condos, and co-ops. Existing homes account for a larger share of the market than new homes and indicate housing market trends. January data is reported on February 23.

## You should be watching:

The GSE reform debate between the Obama administration and Republicans could provide discourse to the markets in February. As I've stated before, any major reform is likely to be pushed off until after the 2012 presidential election.

Just how resilient is the U.S. consumer as we enter the historically frugal months of January, February, and March? The January report showed an increase of 0.6% (0.5% less autos) month to month, from November to December.

I'm starting to pay more attention to a variety of housing indicators. The housing market has been in an L-shaped recovery, which, in addition to low unemployment, has acted as a mild drag to the recovering economy. I'll be on the watch for any signs of vulnerability. See also Existing Home Sales and S&P/Case-Shiller HPI.

Industrial production, which rose 0.8% in January (on the December data), has been particularly strong throughout late 2009 and 2010. Industrial production strength, along with that of ISM manufacturing and motor vehicle sales, is something we need to monitor closely as it is a necessary component of the continuing recovery.

We are starting to see inflationary concerns in India and China. Will inflation be exported to the U.S.? A common theme in many earnings calls lately is how higher input costs are weighing on bottom lines. I don't view inflation as problematic yet in terms of companies' abilities to expand margins and grow earnings. However, CPI has begun to tick higher and it is still worth keeping an eye on for any upward movement.

As I indicated earlier in this month's calendar, I'm a bit concerned that we may start to see vulnerability in the housing space. This is something I'm keeping an eye on. See also Housing Starts and S&P/Case-Shiller HPI.

Return to Page 1

## February indicators / events of note:

## You should be watching:

**Durable Goods Orders**

This monthly release from the U.S. Commerce Department reflects new orders placed with U.S. manufacturers for immediate and future delivery of factory hard goods, and is an indicator of how busy factories will be to fill those orders. January's data is released on February 24.

Durable goods orders are a leading indicator of industrial production and capital spending. The significance of this report is on par with my overall interest this month in watching for signs of continued strength in the U.S. manufacturing sector, as measured by related indicators such as, but not limited to, industrial production, ISM manufacturing and motor vehicle sales.

**Gross Domestic Product (GDP)**

The quarterly GDP report, released by the U.S. Commerce Department, tracks the purchases of all U.S. goods and services in all sectors and is the broadest measure of the economy. Preliminary GDP for Q4 2010 comes out on February 25.

U.S. GDP is of increasing interest to me. Coming into 2011, analysts' expectations were for GDP to continue to surprise, with estimates in the range of 2.5% to 4%. Let's see if the reported figures are capable of turning expectations into reality this month.

**S&P/Case-Shiller HPI (Home Price Index)**

This index, released on a two-month lag, tracks changes in the value of residential real estate in 20 metropolitan regions across the U.S. December data will be released on February 25.

What's most important to glean from this report is whether home prices are beginning to resume their former decline, which I think right now has the potential to occur. See also Housing Starts and Existing Home Sales.

**Will the Fed Respond Early to Banks' Capital Plans?**

As part of the Fed's enhanced supervisory process over the U.S. banking system, large bank holding companies were required to submit their capital action proposals for 2011 to the Fed in early January, including any plans to reinitiate dividends or implement share repurchases. While the Fed is expecting to respond to bank plans by March 22, there is no hard deadline and it is possible a response could come earlier for some banks, perhaps in February.

The Fed's response, which could come at any time by mid-March, has the potential to be a bullish catalyst for a weak market. The Street would view the news favorably if a large bank passes this latest "stress test" and is allowed to reintroduce its dividend or buy back shares. For this very reason, I would be on the lookout for Fed announcements on this front throughout February.

**China PMI**

China PMI is released on the last day of the month. This monthly gauge of China's manufacturing sector, combined with monthly U.S. ISM Manufacturing Index released the next day, gives a clear picture of global manufacturing health. An index value above 50 indicates growth, below 50 contraction.

China PMI is back on the calendar, coming off Chinese President Hu Jintao's mid-January visit to the White House for the first time since 2006. China's economy continues to heat up with Q4 GDP at 9.8%, up from 9.6% in Q3 and slightly ahead of the Street's expectations. China's central bank recently raised banks' reserve-requirement ratio and potential exists for interest rate hikes in February. Will actions to cool China's economy have the desired effect – and by how much? We will have to wait and see whether China's February manufacturing results contribute to a red close for the month.

# Acknowledgments

I consider myself incredibly blessed. My fondest memories are from my childhood, and there is truly no place like "home." The foundation in which those childhood memories were built was through the sacrifice of my parents. My sister, Linda, and I lost our mom in 1994 and our dad in 2000. Although my parents passed much too young, the foundation they built is what I stand upon today.

Professional success is unattainable without some luck, mentoring, and assistance. I had the good luck to meet Mark Fisher in 1989. For twenty-two years, Mark never gave up on me. "Unconditional"—what else can be asked for in a relationship?

In December 2007, I stepped in to Susan Krakower's office for the first time. Susan is the creator of CNBC's *Fast Money*. Susan didn't just create an entertaining show, she created careers. I am thankful she gave me a chance to be part of *Fast Money*. This book and the professional success I enjoy today would not be possible without Susan.

In addition to my role on *Fast Money*, I also am the chief market strategist for Virtus Investment Partners. Our CEO, George Aylward, defines our mission as "unwavering commitment to investor success." I feel privileged to follow George's leadership. Jeff Cerutti, our executive vice president, is the creative force behind much of the market commentary I provide. Also at Virtus, my gratitude to Michael Angerthal, Pete Batchelar, Sharon Bray-Chaffee, Joe Fazzino, Lisa Fydenkevez, Matt Hamel, Lynn Kochanski, John McCormack, Emma Simon, Janet Wajda, Frank Waltman, and the entire sales team.

CNBC CEO Mark Hoffman allows me each night to share my day in the market with the viewers. I shall never take that responsibility lightly and will continue to follow the standards of excellence that Mark has set for CNBC. John Melloy is the executive producer for *Fast Money*, and from 5:00 p.m. to 6:00 p.m. he is the conductor. John is incredibly creative and helps us blend market content with entertainment value. Melissa, Guy, Timmy, Karen, and Pete tolerate me each night (sorry and thank you). Mary Duffy always told me "you can" even when I doubted I could.

My appreciation to the following colleagues and contributors at CNBC: Andy Barsh, Marc Briganti, Nik Deogun, Nick Dunn, David Faber, Jason Farkas, Courtney Gartman, Dennis Gartman, Beth Goldman, Steve Grasso, Simon Hobbs, Ron Insana, Gary Kaminsky, Brian Kelly, Max Meyers, Jon Najarian, Ariel Nelson, Joanne O'Brien, James Sannella, Anthony Scaramucci, Lori Spechler, Brian Steel, Lydia Thew, Scott Wapner, and Andy Yonteff.

Too often we forget where we come from, and I have been blessed with great teachers and friends along the way. I was fortunate to attend and graduate from Chaminade High School, an all-boys school in Mineola, New York. Many of the character traits that have made me a success in business—my work ethic, my commitment to excellence, my ability to organize and synthesize information—were forged there. Just as Chaminade helped make me the man I am today, MBF helped make me the market strategist I am today. From 1990 to 2008, I learned so much about investing from the success and failures of so many people at MBF. My approach to the market today is the culmination of that experience. First and foremost among the MBF gang is Rob Michiels, whom I consider "my brother." Contributors to my success also include Adam Benner, Tony Birbillis, Eric Bolling, Barry Charles, Bucky

DeMarco, Scott Edwards, Baruch Glaubach, Steve Goldberg, Sandy Goldfarb, Evan Halpern, Lou Hazan, William Keeney, John McCann, Charlie McGuffog, Tom Schiff, Jeffrey Schondorf, Charles Weisman, and David Yankovich.

To my family and friends who have supported me in good times and bad: my wife, Tiffany; my children, Tucker, Tanner, and Remy; my sister, Linda, and her family, Glenn, Lilli, and Tyler; my in-laws, Yoli and Al.

Peter Ferraro has dealt with my many moods as we have driven much of the tristate area together; thanks, Pete. Mike Bossy's friendship and advice means so much to me. My gratitude for the invaluable friendships of Nick Cacciatore, Pete and Peggy Cossu, Daniel Fisher, Jessica Fisher, Mike Handel, Justin Johnson, Gary and Lori Kaminsky, George Mellilo, Rob and Debbie Michiels, Barry Platnick, Mike and Andi Schorr, Ralph Sellitti, Brett and Meri Votano, and Joe Theismann.

The production of this book benefitted from the collaborative efforts of Jeffrey Krames. I also thank Kelli Christiansen for her assistance during the editing process. My editor, John Brodie, from the very first day believed in me, and he worked constantly behind the scenes to help make this a better book. I will always be grateful to John for his considerable contributions to this project.

To all of you, long health and happiness!

# Index

Stop loss limit 200

2.00 — move it to
400.00

Tax loss.

**BUSINESS
PLUS**

Recognized as one of the world's most prestigious business imprints, Business Plus specializes in publishing books that are on the cutting edge. Like you, to be successful we always strive to be ahead of the curve.

Business Plus titles encompass a wide range of books and interests—including important business management works, state-of-the-art personal financial advice, noteworthy narrative accounts, the latest in sales and marketing advice, individualized career guidance, and autobiographies of the key business leaders of our time.

Our philosophy is that business is truly global in every way, and that today's business reader is looking for books that are both entertaining and educational. To find out more about what we're publishing, please check out the Business Plus blog at:

**www.bizplusbooks.com**